"This writing business.
Pencils and what-not.
Over-rated, if you ask me.
Silly stuff.
Nothing in it."

Eeyore from Winnie the Pooh

What a pleasure this book is! For those taking their tentative first steps along "The Path," Michael Sharp outlines clearly, concisely, and in no uncertain terms some of the critical basic (and not so basic) steps appropriate to incorporate into your daily routine in order to facilitate your process. For the rest of us, it's still a more-than-worthwhile refresher course—I caught myself saying, "Oh, yeah, that's right...how did I forget to do that every day?" more than once, and I've been doing this for a while! Definitely a must-have in every aspiring ascender's library!
Deb, SunDiskScribes

I have read authors from Chopra to Ruiz to Weiss; I have gone to every kind of holistic therapy imaginable. I have searched and questioned and researched. The turning point came when *What the Bleep* was released here.... I literally sat in the cinema and cried with relief. Then I was led to Wallace D. Wattles. From there came *The Secret* and then Bill Harris with his Holo-Sync program. Then I watched *The Mayan Calendar and the Transformation of Consciousness*. And now there's you, Michael Sharp. **C.D.**

Dear Michael, you really are a gift, and I honor you Dr. Michael Sharp! You are a true Ascension Master and I am very grateful for your wisdom and presence here. **Nate**

Got all your books and have finished the first two. I am nearly finished *The Book of Light*—brilliant—thank-you! It has really opened a remembrance and a place of being that was forgotten—never have I experienced such a concise explanation for our existence—and I have read a lot!!!
Margie (South Africa)

After pondering the messages in Michael Sharp's books I discovered a rather profound realization. The human race is constantly looking backwards. Have you been searching for ancient wisdom, researching long standing religions, joining secret societies, traveling the planet for clues, or practicing methods and techniques pasted down from our ancestors? There is a very common belief that the wisdom of the ages can be accessed by looking into the messages of the past but I would like to suggest there is another way. The new belief is that **you** have the capability to establish the same connection to an all-knowing consciousness that the ancient prophets and masters utilized. This point in time is unique and you no longer need to look any further than your own personal spiritual instinct. *Michael's material is designed to stretch your awareness, expand your consciousness, shift your limiting belief system, clear your emotional blocks, balance your feminine and masculine aspects, reawaken your non-physical sense, and generally give you simple techniques to create a quiet and peaceful mind. I know the laundry list of items mentioned above sounds crazy from a human perspective, but I have experienced all of that and more. These books are spot on.*
Rod Nelson

Dearest Michael, I have finished reading the first part of your *Book of Light*. Thank you. I was never able to conceptualize this pattern before now. I have been in this body almost fifty years. I have traveled the globe in search for clue's into my divinity. I have watched myself swim in the Amazon basin, trekked the mountains of Peru, entered the sacred caves with the Mayan of Guatemala, walked the path of Jesus through Jerusalem, and touched the energy of his birth. Now I know what I was trying to remember. Now after everything has been spent, at the edge of my created small self, I can look up into eternity. I hope one day to meet you, in body or spirit, at the speed of thought. Again I thank you. This day before Christmas, this day after my dear friend sent this link to me, this day of my realization. I love you for writing this. I love myself because I know we are one. **Kathy St. Onge**

I have read your Book of Life and at the moment I am reading The Dossier. I wish to thank you for your work. I have been reading and searching for answers for years and only since reading your books can I make sense of this world. **Mary Mcleod**

Dear Michael, I just want to express my gratitude for your profound words and magnificent works of art. You take my breath away and touched my spirit more than anything that I have come across in my search for truth. I bow to your magnificence, which in turn is bowing to myself. With great respect and utmost love. **Lily**

Michael, I have been reading your books for a little over a year now and frankly, I've never seen anything as clear and enlightening as this. I am very grateful to have connected with this Creation. **Joel B.**

Dear Michael, I just want to send off a note of gratitude for the awesome (no other way to describe it!) contribution you have made to my personal evolution with your books. I had been actively requesting new spiritual information, and one day, wham, up on my screen from Amazon appears your books. Read them all and loved them, then passed them on to my friends who rave about them as well. Can't wait to get your new book, as I'm sure it will be as powerfully packed as your others. Espavo, **Theresa**

Thank you, Michael. I have read your first two books and have just ordered two more. Despite having been on "The Path" for many years (since the early 70's), these books put everything together for me like no other information I have come across; and trust me, I have read hundreds of books. **Jeweline B.**

Dear Michael, I purchased *The Book of Life* and received *The Book of Light* at the same time from your website and could not put the books down—they were so enthralling! I also bought *The Dossier of the Ascension* and *The Book of the Triumph of Spirit* and again read expectantly. Your works are truly amazing and are helping my husband and I move in quantum leaps forward spiritually through your suggested practices. We have both been on a spiritual path we love for 25 years, but I did not know how to welcome my "True Self" or "lift The Veil" until you. *Your works have liberated me*! We both thank you for your dedicated efforts. **Anonymous.**

THE GREAT AWAKENING

Concepts and Techniques
For Successful Spiritual Practice

by

Dr. Michael Sharp

www.michaelsharp.org
www.crystalchildrenbooks.com

Avatar Publications
A Division of Immortality Inc.
www.avatarpublication.com

An Avatar Book

Published by Avatar Publications

St Albert, Alberta. Canada

www.avatarpublication.com

For information on bulk purchase discounts contact

Avatar Publications at sales@avatarpublication.com

Library of Congress Cataloging-in-
Publication Data

Sharp, Michael, 1963-
 The great awakening : concepts and
techniques for successful spiritual practice
/ by Michael Sharp.
 p. cm.
 Includes index.
 ISBN 978-1-897455-74-6 (alk. paper) -- ISBN
978-1-897455-75-3 (ebook)
 1. Spiritual life--Miscellanea. I. Title.

 BF1999.S4383 2007
 204'.4--dc22
 2007033585

TABLE OF CONTENTS

DEDICATIONS

TO MY WIFE

If you live to be a hundred,
I want to live to be a hundred minus one day,
so I never have to live without you.
Winnie the Pooh

TO MY KIDS

If there ever comes a day
when we can't be together,
keep me in your heart,
I'll stay there forever.
Winnie the Pooh

TO THE WORLD

If you want to make a song more hummy,
add a few tiddely poms.
Winnie the Pooh

PART ONE:
ROAD SCHOOL

AWAKENING AND EMPOWERMENT

"What does Crustimoney Proseedcake mean?" said Pooh. For I am a Bear of Very Little Brain, and long words bother me.

~ Winnie the Pooh

Greetings, dear reader, and welcome. My name is Michael Sharp and the book in your hand is the key to your rapid and safe spiritual awakening and empowerment. This book is a spiritual primer. As mentioned on the back cover, this book provides the foundational materials for the Great Awakening—i.e., the individual and collective return of Christ Consciousness to this planet. This book provides <u>all</u> the basic information you need. Here you will find information on breathing, visualization, intent, and other concepts and techniques critical for effortless progress forward into the new spiritual millennium. Here you will find everything you need in order to *initiate* a successful awakening experience. Where you go from this initiation will be up to you.

I would like to say at the outset that no matter where you are on your own spiritual path, this book will be useful. It is my strong advice that you not overlook the concepts and ideas presented here no matter how skilled or knowledgeable you might be. Just because this book functions as an introduction to my work, doesn't mean it contains only simple information or that the information here is optional. The materials presented are important. If you are going to make good progress on your return path back home, if you are going to wake up with speed and facility, you need to know the basics as presented in this book in some form or another. Learn the concepts here or learn them from someone else. It doesn't matter. Just learn them.

I would also like to say that although the information set forth here will be useful for all people interested in a rapid return to full consciousness, this book will be particularly useful for those of you who have previous religious or scientific training, those of you who come from judgmental spiritual backgrounds,[1] and those of you who are experiencing **disorientation or anxiety** over personal or collective events. To you, a special welcome! I promise you, you will find the material in this book (indeed in all my *Lightning Path*[2] books) will go a long way towards providing you calm, clarity of vision when it comes to your own

----

[1] That is, from **all** those belief systems that emphasize reward and punishment, karma, retribution, and other forms of soul-to-soul violence.

[2] The *Lightning Path* is my name for my "system" of rapid spiritual awakening. The system consists of books and poems designed to move your consciousness forward into full knowledge and acceptance of the divinity within with speed, efficiency, and safety. More information, and a complete list of Lightning Path Books, can be found at the back of this book.

efforts to "sort through" the things happening in your world.

Let me also be clear that neither this book, nor any of my books, for that matter, is a book about spiritual "enlightenment." This is not a book about soul evolution, spiritual evolution, consciousness "raising," karmic work, "altitude" or anything ridiculous like that. This is not a book about how to "save" yourself or others and it is certainly not a book of commandments or morality.

This is a book about awakening and ***nothing*** more.

This is a book about awakening your mind and your body and empowering into the **full light** of your full and glorious spiritual consciousness without compromise and with no strings attached.

Now, perhaps at this point you are curiously asking yourself, "Why awakening and not enlightenment, salvation, or evolution as the masons, priests, or scientists might say?"

If so, good question!

It is for two reasons.

On the one hand, it is because the notions of enlightenment, salvation, and evolution have way too much baggage attached to them to be useful. When you get down to the nitty-gritty of it, there are literally centuries of dogma and misconception attached to the "standard" explanations of our origin and purpose (i.e., we are here to evolve, to become enlightened, to learn, to work off karmic "debt," blah, blah). To be blunt, there are centuries of lies about enlightenment, salvation, and evolution floating around in that collective consciousness of ours. As such, there is just too much *crap* attached to these concepts for them to be of any use at all.

On the other hand, the other reason why we don't want to use words like enlightenment, salvation, or evolution to describe this process is that despite all the millions of words creatively wasted on these concepts, the process I talk about in this book (and in all my books) really is a process of awakening. It is not about enlightenment, karmic resolution, salvation, soul healing, evolution, testing, judgment, or any of the other (often millennial) nonsense you hear from the "doomsayers," "prophets," and self-styled messengers of this world. The process I talk about really is a process of awakening. It is a process of returning your full consciousness to your physical body and mind and nothing more.

That is all there is to it.

In fact, when I think about this "Great Awakening," this process of collective and individual *return to glory,* I think it is very much like the normal cycle of sleep and awakening you go through every day.

Every day is the same.

Every cycle is the same.

Every night you go to sleep and "descend" into a state of reduced consciousness. In that state, you are operating at reduced capacity. Your mind is numb, your senses are turned off, and your bodily systems respond only to emergency. However, every morning when you are rested, or when you, somebody you love, or somebody that you asked to awaken you, *brrriiiiiiiinnnngggsss* an alarm clock close to your head, you wake up. You open your eyes, struggle back to "full" consciousness, and go about your daily work at "full" capacity with eyes "wide open" and consciousness "fully present" with no trouble at all.

Awakening is easy. In fact, you have been doing it every day since you were born, right? And although sometimes getting out of bed can be extremely difficult (especially if you are sick or have had a rough night), you always succeed at it sooner or later.

Easy peasy lemon squeezy.

It is exactly the same way with this spiritual awakening process that I am talking about, although for the sake of explanatory power we extend the metaphor a bit and shift our perception of the physical body. Thus, instead of identifying with your physical body as if it is a part of the "I" that is you, see your body/mind as a *container* for your consciousness. View your body/mind as a vehicle for your soul, a temple for your spirit. Know that it is a very good vehicle; an excellent vehicle, in fact. Indeed, your body/mind combination it is a finely tuned, precision-engineered powerhouse of creation.[3] Your body is a fantastic vehicle for your soul; that is for sure. However, despite its sophistication and power, it also a very fragile vehicle. Not only must your body survive, revive, and regenerate from the daily insults of life on this earth, it must also cope with the inferno of your spiritual consciousness. To your body, which is crystallized, frozen energy, your soul is literally fire. The fire of your soul, which is necessary to animate your body, nevertheless strains the crystallized, ice-like molecular structures of your brain/body to the point of failure. Because of that, and because of the insults and toxins and other physical difficulties, every night your body and mind must rest to recover, regenerate, and repair.

Simple, right?

In order to facilitate the regeneration of your body, your consciousness exits its mortal coil every night and goes cavorting out and about the multi-verse. As your consciousness does this, as a greater proportion of your animating soul leaves your body,

---

[3] See my *Dossier of the Ascension* for a more detailed explanation of the powerhouse that is your soul's physical temple.

your body goes to sleep. While sleeping, it repairs itself. Ideally, when it's done its repair, consciousness comes back and your body wakes up.

When sleeping, the body/mind is *almost* empty of consciousness. It cannot be fully empty because if it was, if your consciousness completely left your body, your body would immediately die. Thus, in order to preserve the physical integrity of the cellular structure of your body, your consciousness retains a thin connection to it.[4] However for the most part, consciousness leaves the body alone so it can recover in peace.[5] If you want a number, we

---

[4] Some people call this connection your "astral cord" but that image is really a metaphoric representation of a more complex relationship between soul and body. Technically, your spirit *envelops* the cells of your body. Thus when sleeping, there is a diminished level of envelopment.

[5] The dreaming that we do at night is a dim, heavily filtered, and often symbolically obscured echo of the activity of our spiritual consciousness as it goes out and cavorts in the multi-verse. If you are interested, it is possible to improve the connection and remember more of what goes on. That is, it is possible to train your body/mind to keep a stronger connection to your soul. If you achieve this, your body/mind will remember (with greater or lesser clarity) where your soul has been and what it has been doing.

A lot of people, when they begin to go through their awakening process, do in fact begin to connect with the activities of their soul and do begin to remember what's going on during the night. In the early, ungrounded stages, this can mean weird dreams and disturbed sleep patterns. In general, I don't recommend this and would actively discourage "night travels" of this type at any point in your awakening. It is important that your body and brain get

could say that only about two percent (2%) of your consciousness inhabits your body while it is sleeping. Of course, the percentage of consciousness changes when you wake up in the morning. In the morning, when your body and mind are rested and recovered, your consciousness returns more fully to your body. Not too much though. For reasons explained elsewhere,[6] under "normal" conditions, only about ten percent (10%) of your full consciousness re-enters your body/mind when you wake up. This is not too much and in reality represents a serious diminishment of your full capacity. This minimal ten percent makes the "waking you," what society and psychologists would call the "normal" you, a mere shadow of who you *really* are.[7] The ten percent is enough for you to function properly[8] in the "energy extraction systems" of this world, but it does not represent anywhere near your full capacity. In truth, it represents a sort of semi-conscious sleepwalking with a sort of semi-intelligence, semi-awareness.

Truth is, "normal" isn't very much of you at all.

---

proper rest at all times. As we shall see below, proper rest will be even more important as you initiate and progress through the awakening process.

[6] See my *Book of Life: Ascension and the Divine World Order* and *The Book of Light: The Nature of God, the Structure of Consciousness, and the Universe Within You.* You can find details on where to get the books at the back of this book.

[7] Plato talked about this with his cave metaphor, but in a clumsy, heavily veiled sort of way.

[8] That is, efficiently and without complaint.

Truth is, there is a vast potential in you that lies unrealized and untapped.

If you want, you can consider the previous Avatar Jesus Christ as an exemplar of the possibilities open to a fully awakened, fully conscious human mind/body.[9]

Pretty exciting when you think about it.

So **why** are you sleepwalking through life and **how** do you wake up and access full capacity? The answer to the question of "why" is provided in my *Book of Life: Ascension and the Divine World Order,* so I won't rehearse that answer here. As to how you wake up, it is not that hard at all and, in fact, that is what this book is for. In these pages I will provide guidance on getting the process rolling. More importantly, I will show you that, contrary to what some

---

[9] For the sake of accuracy, and to avoid any possible misconception, Christ's miraculous abilities required two things. The first was a fully awakened, fully empowered human body. The second was an "ascended" space. Back when Christ walked the earth, the Twelve Apostles provided the *lift* that made Christ's space "ascended." Do not forget this. You can't expect "easy magic" to happen in a space that is not ascended. Not to worry, though. As you will learn when you read *The Book of Life: Ascension and the Divine World Order,* we (and by we I mean everybody on this earth) are currently working on creating a universal ascended space were we, as fully awakened, fully empowered human beings, are going to create a new Eden, a new cosmic Shambhala. We should be done "the dirty work" by 2012, at which time "*the magic*" should become quite obvious to anybody who isn't totally comatose.

might like to tell you, the process of awakening is not that hard at all. In fact, it takes only a little bit of time, willingness, and effort. How long it will take, and how much effort you will need to expend, will depend largely on you and your own unique situation. Bottom line, some of you will find it easy to wake up and others will have more difficulty. However, don't make anything of that. Awakening is not a question of talent or worthiness or grace. It really just depends on conditions in your life, but even in the worst case (i.e., hard nights, bad nightmares, illness, heavy grogginess, unsupportive environment, and moderate-to-severe disorientation), a couple of years is all you need *if* you stay focused and if you practice the techniques provided in this, and subsequent, books. Not that hard at all, especially considering what you might have been told by others. What's even better, there is a nice bonus at the end of it all. Once you're finished this process, you won't have any more need for psychologists, integral theorists, prophets, pundits, or any of the others whose job is to "save your soul" or "improve you" in some way. I'm the last "prophet" you'll ever need. I'll teach you you're perfect already and, when you finally, *really* realize that, you'll be done. At that point you'll be moving forward under your own steam, gathering your own information from God and Spirit, making your own creative decisions, and manifesting the conditions you want to manifest with confidence and aplomb. It might not be good for the long-term financial health of the healing and self-help industries, but what can I say. The trees of this earth will thank you.

In closing this chapter on the idea of spiritual awakening, let me be perfectly clear so there is no potential misunderstanding. Awakening in the spiritual sense, i.e., awakening from ten percent to one hundred percent, is exactly like the "normal" awakening you do every morning. It is exactly like going from two percent to ten percent, which is to say, it *is* just like getting out of bed in the morning. It is a simple matter of **intent** and **persistence**. When you wake up in the morning you do not have to run races, pass tests, or "prove your worth" in order to get out of bed. **You just get up**. As we shall see in more detail in the next chapter, it is the same with spiritual awakening. There is no entrance fee, no judgment at the door, no pearly gates, no gatekeeper, no test of worthiness, no complicated curriculum, no final exam, no nothing. It doesn't even matter what you have done in this or any past life. The truth is, your soul could be black as coal and you still get to wake up and walk back into The Garden[10] for a nice cup of tea, just like that.

No questions asked.

No strings attached.

You just need to get up.

You just need to wake up.

So wake up!

---

[10] See my *Parable of the Garden* at the back of this book.

And wake up others!![11]

The time is fast approaching.

The *transitioning* of 2012 is almost upon us.

So wake up!!!

Embrace the global return of higher consciousness.

Embrace the global return of higher self.

Embrace this global return of Christ.

Embrace The Great Awakening!

It is going to be quite glorious and I promise you the world is going to change, and for the better, rapidly, and in quite dramatic ways, *despite what the doomsayers are saying* and despite any doubts you might have. To the un-awakened, it is going to look like magic, but don't let the magic fool you. As you will learn from this and subsequent books, *The Great Awakening* is a carefully orchestrated event that we (and by we I mean the six billion people on this earth and the other 36 billion or so disincarnated guides and helpers) have been preparing for, for over one hundred thousand years. So embrace it without hesitation and without reservation!

From this point on, there is nothing to fear.

---

[11] Give them this free eBook or a copy of the print version. Share far and wide!

Now, let us start this process immediately, shall we? Let us begin, in the next chapter, with the necessary first step of getting rid of any misconceptions about spirituality that you might have absorbed while sleepwalking through this, or previous, lifetimes on this earth. Once these misconceptions, these "obstacles" to your spiritual awakening, are out of the way we will move onto a discussion of basic bodily techniques for safe awakening and empowerment. Through all of this remember, this a basic book. None of the stuff we discuss here will be difficult to understand or disconcerting to your soul[12] and everything will be meted out in easy to absorb and integrate chunks.

As a final word before moving on, I certainly expect the information here to be of practical benefit to you. In fact, as you practice what I preach, you should begin to notice immediate changes, some subtle, some not so subtle, in your life and your state of consciousness. Pay attention to those changes, embrace them, welcome them with joy (because they mean a better life is on the way) and when

---

[12] Unless, perhaps, you are recently coming from a fundamentalist background, in which case you might have considerable difficulty with this book. If you do find yourself having difficulties with these materials, review the chapter on *trust* in this book and try to put aside the fire and brimstone, judgmental and threatening exhortations fed to you by the pulpit bangers within your particular flavor of fundamentalism. *Trust me.* I'm not here to trick you into damnation or steal your soul. I'm here to help free your soul.

they begin to accelerate, don't get freaked out. Some of the changes may feel dramatic and earth shattering, at least on "that side" of the meniscus,[13] but they are not. They only look that way. After a little bit of effort and progress, the changes you go through won't seem so very big at all, so embrace the changes. And if things are moving too fast, remember, you are in control of this process. You initiated the process by picking up this book and engaging in the practices outlined here and you can control the speed simply through intent. Move as fast or as slow as you want. Take whatever time you need to integrate and process and hey, if you need to snooze a little longer, if you find this all too weird and discombobulating, and if there isn't anybody in immediate physical danger around you, feel free to snooze a little longer.

We'll all manage just fine until you are ready.

I'll warn you though, you can only hit the snooze button for so long.

After 2012, you got to wake up.

Just so you know...

You can't stay sleeping forever.

---

[13] Merriam-Webster Online defines meniscus as *the curved upper surface of a column of liquid*. The meniscus is the "skin" on the top of the water. It's the think layer that the bugs float on beneath which extends the vast ocean of consciousness.

RIGHT THINKING

"Yes," said Winnie-the-Pooh.

"I see now," said Winnie-the-Pooh.

"I have been Foolish and Deluded,"

said he, "and I am a Bear of no

Brain at All."

As I said in the last chapter, before we get into the practical advice and technique section of this book, I first want to clear the ground of any misconceptions you may have about what it means to be a spiritual person. I do not want to get into a lengthy debate with myself (or you) here, so I will assume you are prepared to at least consider what I have to say. Therefore, I will provide a short list of misconceptions, without argument or justification. If you want confirmation of the truths I tell you, you can get it by just asking for it (see the section on communicating with Spirit later in this book). Put the question out to the universe and Spirit will provide.

Of course, I realize there may be some resistance to what I have to say here. Some of you may be just starting out, you may be coming from dogmatic backgrounds, or you may not have a big picture view yet, so it may not be immediately clear why I identify one idea or another as a misconception or error. If you do feel yourself resisting (but you still want to move forward), don't fret too much about it. Don't kick yourself over it. You can let go of your resistance whenever you feel comfortable doing so. I'm not asking you to throw all your old ideas out and operate on blind faith. I'm also not threatening you in any way (i.e., you're not going to burn in hell or be reborn as a slug for not "following the rules"). I'm just asking you to try these ideas on for size for a bit and see if they don't lead you towards an obvious awakening, an easily recognizable expansion of consciousness. If you find these ideas are not leading you towards a positive spirituality and a positive empowerment, feel free to stick with what works for you. You can always come back and try it on for size at a later date.

The door will always be open.

However, I will say this: No matter what you do, it is important to understand (even at this early stage) that your ideas about spirituality *determine* your experience of spirituality and even your experience of life. If you believe in a spirituality of judgment, damnation, competition, struggle, and strife, don't be surprised if you experience these things in "reality." You create the world around you through the ideas that you have in your head. If you have "old world" ideas and old world spiritual conceptions, you will create, live in, and die in an old world of duality, conflict, and strife. You can do that if you want. However, if you want to awaken from that old world nightmare and see what's really possible, read on. This is the way forward.

Misconception One: *Being Spiritual means you are broken. You are damaged in some way. You need to be fixed. You ate some bad fruit and were thrown out of The Garden. You*

27

are a bad little boy or girl and you don't listen. You are full of sin and need to be constantly directed and punished. You are souls in bodily evolution (or is that bodies in soul evolution?) and you must struggle through lifetimes of pain and despair in order to attain perfection of DNA, of spirit, of whatever. You are children, sinful, dirty, disgusting, un-evolved, and descended.

Well, listen...

I'm here to tell you, these things are not true.

Here is the truth:

You are not descended from apes.

You are not souls in training.

You are not evolving from mud.

You are not broken angels.

You are not weak.

You are not sinful.

You are not cast-outs from The Garden.

In fact, you are not broken in any way and you are certainly not in any need of salvation.

The real story, which I talk about in more detail in subsequent books (and also see The Parable of the Garden at the back of this book), is much more glorious and grand than all that nonsense. The real story is you, me, and everyone on this planet are on a mission. The real story is, we have undertaken a Divine task. We are working on God's Plan and in order to accomplish that plan we have, for a long time, been walking around in "darkness." We have had a "veil" placed on our bodies' minds that has prevented, up until now, more than ten percent of our full spiritual consciousness from entering the physical body. In other words, we have been asleep, but for a reason!

Now, you don't need me to tell you, it has been a tough slog. We have had to put up with a lot of shit and abuse while sleeping through our mission.

I will be the first to acknowledge that.

We have endured the pain.

However, no sense in getting worked up over it. It will be worth it; you'll see. As we will find out, the thing that we have accomplished, the thing that we have worked towards, the "ascension of the universe," as it is called, is grand, glorious, magnificent and definitely worth the trouble.

You'll see.

Misconception Two: *Spirituality is like one big test so you better study, work hard, do your homework, polish your shoes, clear your karma, learn, evolve, hope, and pray that when the time comes for judgment you will pass "the test" and be found worthy, strong, intelligent, good, genetically fit, or whatever.*

But listen…

You can give that nonsense up right now.

The truth is, your life is not a classroom, this earth is not a school, and your goal is not to pass some kind of cosmic final exam. The truth is, you are not on this earth to prove your worthiness or win your way back into God's good graces. The truth is, you are not here to pass some karmic test or learn to be good little boys and girls. Spirit exists forever and when you die you are not judged, stamped, and sent to the "appropriate karmic level." When you die, all that happens is that you take another body (or not, depending on what you want to do) and are reborn into a situation of **your choosing**.

It is important you understand this, so pay attention.

Nobody makes you take a body.

Nobody tells you where to incarnate.

Nobody sets a plan for you.

Nobody judges your sins and nobody (not even God) tells you where to go, what "lessons" to learn, or what you should experience.

As immortal Spirit, whatever you want to do, wherever you want to go, whatever you want to experience, and whomever you want to be is your choice.

No judgment.

No strings attached.

It's all up to you.

It's all within your power. So, keep this in mind and, from this point forward, make the choices that are right for you and the ones you love.

Misconception Three: *Being spiritual means being submissive. Spirituality requires submission to an authority figure of some sort. Bow low and be humble, little one. Submit and be good little lambs. Do what you are told or old St. Nick will bring you what you deserve on Christ's Birthday. Do not disobey or St. Peter won't let you in through the Pearly Gates. Do not rebel or you will be cast out. Do not sin against God or you will be damned to eternal hell fire.*

Rubbish. Rubbish. Rubbish.

Truth is, doing what you are told doesn't make you a spiritual person, a good person, or a holy person.

It doesn't make you a bad person, either.

It just makes you a person that does what you are told to do for whatever reason that is.

That's all.

It goes no deeper than that, so don't expect some kind of reward or punishment for following authority, or not. You create the reality you experience through the choices you make and you (and others, of course) live with the consequences of your choices. It is as simple as that.

Now of course, this doesn't mean you can go out and do whatever you want to do. You have to remember that your actions, <u>even your thoughts</u>, have consequences for you, for others. It's always your choice; but, take responsibility for <u>ALL</u> your actions. You are not children. If you want to go jump around in the mud, be prepared to do your own cleanup work. Take responsibility! Own up to your actions. If you get drunk, get behind the wheel and kill somebody, you're responsible. If you push a button that drops a bomb that kills a thousand people, you're responsible. If you hurt your spouse, or damage your children emotionally, physically, or spiritually, you're responsible. If you muck up someone else's life because of your action (or inaction), you're responsible.

If you do that, you have to make amends.

You have to atone.

Now, if you want my advice, you want to avoid making messes and mucking around with others lives because, bottom line, you're responsible for the messes you create. As you wake up, you will feel yourself accountable for cleaning up and you will not make progress forward until you accept responsibility and atone for your "sins." Believe me, you can save yourself a lot of head banging if you stop making messes immediately.

Remember, it doesn't matter whether you are following authority or not. It is the consequences of your actions that you are responsible for. If you take actions that are hurtful to others, then you've hurt others. If you make a decision that leaves people homeless, if you start a war and drop a bomb, if you encourage a crusade, if you steal from the poor, if you rape a child, you've hurt somebody.

Of course, no fully conscious immortal soul is going to stand in judgment of your actions, but at the same time, as you wake up, we are all going to expect you to clean up the messes that you've left. If you want my advice, instead of living in fear of punishment and/or anticipation of reward, instead of worrying about doing what the authorities tell you to do, start paying attention to the real impact of your actions.

And don't get me wrong. I'm not wagging my finger at you here. I don't want you to dwell on what you've done in the past or feel guilty.

The past is done. Atone in equal measure to your "sin," atone until that "little voice inside" says you're done, and then forget about it and move on. That's all. From this point on, stand up, take responsibility for your actions, and do the right thing.

Do more than "do unto others."

Uplift, heal, and empower this planet and the people on it. Not only will this help you speed through your own awakening process, but you'll feel a whole lot better about yourself and the world you live in. I guarantee it.

Misconception Four: *Being spiritual means karma, judgment, damnation, and retribution. There are consequences for failure. If you mess up, you're going to be punished. If you screw up, you'll go to jail (hell). You'll be put into a work camp. You'll go to purgatory. You'll be karmically reborn as a slug or maybe (as I heard one catholic priest say on television once), your soul will be* *snuffed out and your naughty little existence terminated like the worthless piece of cosmic turd that you are.*

<u>Snake Oil!</u>

The truth is, there is no such thing as hell or purgatory.

Even the idea of it is senseless.

There is no gatekeeper at the Pearly gates. St. Nick isn't keeping a list, he's not checking it twice, and he certainly doesn't care whether you have been naughty or nice.

The truth is, your worst enemy, the person that you hate the most, the person who has done you wrong a million times through ten hundred thousand lifetimes retains, even now, even after death, exactly the same rights and privileges as you do. It simply doesn't matter what you think about them or what kind of "justice" you think exists in the universe. It ain't gonna happen. We all retain exactly the same rights, privileges, and entitlements no matter who we are, what we've done, or where we've been.

Now, if the thought of this makes you angry, tough.

Hatred and anger, the desire for vengeance, the need to see somebody else in pain, these are the nightmares of a sleeping body. They don't belong in a fully awakened existence.

They won't fit.

In fact, the two are mutually exclusive. You see, your spiritual consciousness is all about love and inclusion and expansiveness and giving. The truth is, your higher self is a glorious beacon of light and love and it cannot abide the negativity of this world. The truth is, our higher self cannot get close to all the negative nonsense we keep percolating in our noodles. If it does, it burns. Therefore, bottom line, if your mind is full of hate, judgment, hierarchy, and suffering, you won't be able to wake up. Your consciousness won't be able to enter. It would simply be in too much pain.

Sorry to say, but that's the way it is. As long as the Jews hate the Arabs and the Arabs hate the American's and the American's hate Al Quaeda and we all hate each other, nobody is waking up. It is impossible. With that much hatred (and fear, for that matter) floating around, ten percent is about as much pain as your soul can handle. If you want my advice, let go of hatred, anger, vengeance, judgment, and ideas about wrath and damnation and let the healing begin so that consciousness may enter and blossom.

Let negativity go.

Release yourself.

"Let him who has cast the first stone" yada, yada, yada.

Forgive and forget.

Golden rules to be sure—deep guidance designed to help you awaken swiftly into full consciousness.

Misconception Five: *Spirituality requires sacrifice and therefore you are going to have to put up with a lot of nonsense in your lifetime if you want to pass "the tests." Suffering and poverty, work and despair, pain and disease, war and violent death are good things for you. What doesn't kill you makes you stronger. You are being tempered in "the fires" of creation. You are a diamond in the rough, a soul in training, so accept and sacrifice.*

But, do I have to say it?

Just in case, I will.

Bullshit!

Truth is, God and Spirit are magnanimous, loving, and expansive. Truth is, there is nothing in any spiritual contract or cosmic document that requires you to put up with any nonsense at all. You don't have to have a disease, you don't have to die early, you don't have to be poor, you don't have to be oppressed, and you don't have to die of starvation (especially considering the abundance of food available on this planet).

God (or god) doesn't want that.

Your higher self doesn't require that.

It's not necessary, not even in the context of the mission we are on.

It just doesn't have to be, so wake up and make a change.

If you find you are putting up with "stuff," I recommend you take steps to stop it. Exercise your God-given right to put your foot down and say, **no more**. Compromise in a healthy and mutually respectful relationship is one thing, but nobody, not even god, requires you to suffer. Like any psychologically healthy and loving parent, god would rather see you joyful, healthy, and alive than in any kind of pain, prison, or purgatory.

So fix what's wrong.

Say to yourself and the world, "No more!!"

Enough, as they say, is enough.

Misconception Six: *It has something to do with how smart you are, how rich you are, how famous you are, how accomplished you are, or how powerful you are. It has something to do with how hard you work, how far you get, or how high you attain. It is a question of your worthiness, of your utility, of your usefulness. Did you listen in school? Did you follow orders? Did you accept and sacrifice? Are you a good boy or girl? Well, then, you'll be rewarded, some day, maybe after you're dead.*

But no, no, no, a thousand times NO.

Being spiritual has nothing to do with how smart you are, how rich you are, how much you attain, how hard you work, or how much you achieve.

It is not about purification, evolution, alchemical transformation to some shiny, but ultimately useless, mineral, or anything like that.

It simply doesn't matter who you are or what you've done. You are no more worthy of health, happiness, wealth, prosperity, and peace than the homeless, jobless, bathless person in the streets of your hometown. In the eyes of God, in the great Unfolding of Spirit, we all deserve prosperity, happiness, peace, love, and desire-no matter what.

To have anything else, to allow anything else to exist, is an affront to our collective divinity. We have accepted it while we've been sleeping, but now that we're waking up, we'll have no more of that nonsense.

Misconception Seven: *Being spiritual is about how "pure" you are, how "egoless" you are, how well you get into a lotus position, how many mushrooms you eat, how well you understand integral philosophy, how many books you've read, etc.*

Oh, my gosh!

Insert any sort of "it's about" clause that you want here, but I'll tell you, whatever you think it means to be spiritual is probably wrong because, and here's the **big revelation**, being spiritual is about nothing at all. The truth is, you are spiritual without even trying. You are already an amazing spiritual light in creation and you don't even have to drag your butt out of bed to be that light.

You don't have to do a darn thing.

You do not have to prove anything.

You don't have to be anybody.

You don't have to go anywhere.

You don't have to serve anyone.

Truth is, nothing that you or I or anybody can say or do changes that fact.

Nothing you say, no mountain you climb, no valley you low, no person you kill, no poor man you spit on, no king that you worship, no good deed that you do, nothing in this great omniverse can make you less than the divine spark of light that you already are.

Truth is, every stinky orifice on your body, every smelly hair beneath your arm, every dirty tooth in your mouth, every etched-in wrinkle on your face, every fuzzy split end on your head, everything about you screams your spirituality and your divinity. Just like going to sleep at night doesn't make you any less of a human being, being "spiritually asleep" doesn't make you any less spiritual. It just means you are asleep.

That's all.

And you know what?

I got great news for you.

The nice thing about all this is, once you get through all these misconceptions and the associated feelings of guilt, shame, unworthiness, and inability that have been programmed into you by "The System" of this earth, you'll find it extremely easy to throw off the cloak of sleep, return to full consciousness, and fix everything that's wrong in your world. All you have to do to get started is put aside the nonsense in your noodle put there by people who don't want you to see your beautiful inner light. So wake up eh. Put aside the nonsense, quit living your life in "darkness," and recapture the awesome glory and light that is you fully awake.

That's all there is to it.

It is not that hard, and in the rest of this book, and, in fact, in all my books, I will assist by providing techniques and information that will help you take not only your first steps, but even your intermediate and advanced steps towards full consciousness. I'd like to start in the next two sections by looking at a couple of things that are important for your spiritual awakening—breathing and visualization. Following that, we will cover other topics like intent, protection of your "spiritual space," conversations with your soul and other important spiritual things like that.

I'm hoping it is going to be an exciting journey of awakening and empowerment for you.

So let's now waste any more time, shall we?

Let us begin.

BREATHING

Before beginning a Hunt, it is wise to ask someone what you are looking for before you begin looking for it.

~ Winnie the Pooh

Hopefully, after reading the last chapter you've taken into consideration some of the things I have said and have taken the first steps towards clearing your consciousness of the damaging dogma of church and science. For reasons that will become clear in this chapter, if you want to move forward, you need to have "right thoughts." If you don't, you may run into some trouble when you face the glorious waters of creation, the deep Fabric of Consciousness, that is your birthright and original state of existence.

In order to explain what I mean by the above, and to kick off the breathing and grounding section of this book, I would like to spend a little time talking about myself and my vision of the world. As you already know, my name is Michael Sharp, and although I fancy myself a bit of spiritual teacher, storyteller, and world teacher, nevertheless I am not special in any way. In fact, I am just like you. I am bundle of describable and indescribable things. I am a Scorpio. I am a parent. I am a partner. I am a worker. I have hair, eyes, teeth, and feet. I have my likes and my dislikes. When I'm pricked, I bleed. If I am poisoned, I die. In every way that is important, I am just like you and just like you I have, from time to time, struggled to understand the world around me. I have looked at the pain and the suffering, the homeless crying and the children dying, the war, the chaos, and the seemingly headlong rush to global destruction and I have said to my self, "Self, what the heck is going on?"

"What is this all about?!"

At one time, my answer to what was going on was that all this, all the lunacy and irrationality of this earth, was the result either of a lunatic, demented God playing some sadistic game of cosmic chess, or was the senseless result of a random, violent evolution. Humans struggling in a universe of evolutionary (if you are scientifically minded) or spiritual (if you are spiritually minded) madness.

Take your pick.

Science version or religious version, it doesn't matter because at one point I realized the awful truth, the visions both come from the <u>same</u> place and because of that, they are both ugly visions.

They are hierarchical visions.

They are exclusionary visions.

They are grotesque and the worst thing about them, they are both totally unconcerned with the horrendous level of suffering that goes down on this earth. In fact, when you stop to look at them closely you see, quite clearly, they both justify the suffering, accept it, and consider it "business as usual."

Spiritual explanations talk about sin, karma, and fallen souls as a justification for suffering. You get the pain in your life because you deserve it in some way. It's either a karmic thing or a "tempering in the fire" thing. You suffer because it's good for you, because it's what god wants, because it's the only way to make you right again after your ignominious "fall" from grace.

Yuck!

Scientific explanations, on the other hand, talk about evolution and survival of the fittest. You're poor, you struggle, you die not because of the twisted social, economic, or political system you live in, and not because of some lunatic, warlord leader, but because you are weak and undeserving. The strong dominate and thrive. The weak serve and suffer. What doesn't' kill ya makes ya stronger.

Ya right!

As you can see, both cases present limited, narrow visions of this universe that we live in, and neither one offers much in the way of a choice. Behind door one you get violent Darwinian struggle. Behind door two you get submission to a sadistic, divine authority that doesn't seem to have a clue.

What kind of choice is this anyway? I mean, both visions suck, and in a big way.

However, happy to say, it is not like that for me anymore. I don't mind saying that nowadays I don't worry about the world at large so much. I have my own personal troubles like everybody else and I deal with them as best I can (I struggle to be a good parent, for example), but when it comes to looking at the larger world and the way it is unfolding, I am at total peace.

You could say that my vision of the world has changed.

Now, don't get me wrong. It is not that I am tuned out to what's happening in this world or that I am unconcerned about the goings on, on this planet.

I am concerned.

It is also not because I don't care about the suffering and the pain that is everywhere around us.

I care deeply.

It is also not because I don't want to work to see a better tomorrow. I absolutely positively do want to see things get better and I absolutely positively am working to create a utopia in this lifetime. It is just that nowadays I see neither a random, evolving universe nor a lunatic and abusive "father figure" in the god seat. Instead, when I look at the world, I see pattern and meaning in all things.

I don't see random evolution or spiritual darkness anywhere.

Instead, I see an expansive and loving God everywhere.

When I look at the world and the people in it, I see the bright light of the creator shining in each and every one of you. When I see the world, I see it as divinely inspired, where Spirit walks and where everything, and I do mean everything, has been under our control since we started this "experiment" way back in the way-gone ages.

Now I admit it, my vision of the world is different than the "normal" vision of the world. I also admit that my vision of the world is a stretch, especially considering the sorry state the world is in these days. Pain and strife, struggle and confusion, war and waste of life are common features of our day-to-day reality. In this context, to think that an expansive and loving God/Spirit is "in control" seems ludicrous. If that was the case, why aren't things any better? I mean, this earth is not exactly what most people would consider the epitome of a divinely inspired, God-given Garden of Eden, is it?

But you know what? That doesn't matter because what you and I see when we see the "normal" vision of reality is only the surface of a much larger reality, with a much deeper purpose and meaning, than we are used to seeing in our "normal" lives. Indeed, the "normal" reality seen by your average, somnambulistic human being is[14] *not even the tip* of the iceberg of what lies "beneath the surface." If I may wax poetic for a moment, what you see when you look at the world around you is merely the meniscus on the water of the consciousness of God. That is, what "normal" people call "normal" reality is merely a "thin crust," beneath which expands a reality so vast and so grand that if you were to poke a hole through that membrane without preparation, if

---

[14] Contrary to Freud and Jung…

you were to even get a glimpse of the "power and the glory" while still caught deep in the maya (i.e., the illusion) of the world, you would experience, depending on the number of erroneous and negative ideas you have about the spiritual universe you live in (see the previous chapter on *Right Thinking*) various levels of discomfort and discombobulation. The truth is, beneath the meniscus that is your work-a-day reality is a reality that is so vast and grand that it boggles the sleeping egoic mind and terrifies the dogmatically straight-jacketed consciousness.

It is the stuff of Annunaki nightmares.

But don't get me wrong.

Don't get all freaked out.

I am not trying to scare you here.

I do not want you to think that the depths of consciousness are too much for you (or anyone) to handle.

Far from it!

Quite the opposite, in fact.

Indeed, let me be the first person to tell you that the reality "beneath the surface," the water that expands into 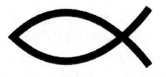 infinity underneath the meniscus, is your *home* reality. That reality, the deep Waters of Creation, as I like to call it, is where you come from and once, not so long ago, you were like a fish, swimming and at home in this vast cosmic ocean of consciousness, as comfortable in the breadth and the depth as a guppy is in a pond.

So what's the problem, then?

Why the attached warning label?

Well, the problem is not that *you* can't handle it (and by you I mean your immortal, conscious soul). The problem is that "you" (and by you I mean your body/mind) can't handle it. The problem is, your waking mind, your bodily mind, that part of you that emerges out of the firing of neuronal synapses, the ego that arises from your brain, is simply out of touch with the power and the glory of its animating consciousness. Let's be honest here. When it comes to things of a spiritual nature, your body/mind, trained as it is in a culture and society that knows next to nothing about spirituality and consciousness, is clueless.

Why?

To make a long story short, you (and by you I mean your body/mind) have been cut off by a socialization and child-rearing process that is decidedly hostile to authentic spirituality and high conscious experience. The problem is that although the vast divine reality was open to you as a child, and although as a child you were comfortable in that reality, as you grew older your understanding of it was never nurtured. In fact, exactly the opposite happened. As you grew up, your understanding, your connection to The Waters, was crushed. As part of the spiritually hostile socialization you received on this world, your connection was severed, smashed, torn apart, ripped asunder, and shredded. You were taught by your parents, by your teachers, and by the media to "leave it behind," to "stay here," and to stay focused in something that "they" (i.e., the people who presumably know about these kinds of things) like to call "reality." You were taught, through constant "tests," punishment, "consequences" and reminders of the precarious nature of your physical existence, to stay focused and present (I would say locked) into "normal." In order to reinforce that disconnection, you were taught to fear "the other side." You were fed silliness about ghosts, goblins, and scary-boo boogey men like the mythological Satan and his army of twisted demon torturers.

All nonsense!

All designed to scare you away from the great pond of consciousness you were able to swim around in as a small child.

Of course, now you don't notice what's missing. You don't notice the fact that your connection to a wider reality, a wide "space" of existence, doesn't exist anymore. It is a frog in boiling water sort of thing. Since "they" get you early, the loss is gradual and unnoticeable. By the time you are an adult (or by the time you attain "adult" status), it is gone and you don't miss it. Sadly, any abilities or sensibilities that you had as a child that were attached to the bigger reality, things like intuition, telepathy, and other nascent skills that need, like language, to be nurtured, are also gone. Like anything, lack of use means atrophy and since the higher reality is closed off from an early age, by the time you are an adult you have no remembered experience, no memory, no left over skills, and no ability to deal with the power and the glory should you inadvertently come into contact with it.

This is the problem.

By the time you are an adult, the deeper reality is as foreign and strange, startling and striking to the narrow consciousness of your egoic mind as life in another universe would be. Stranger, in fact, and, thanks to the priests, pundits and scientists of this planet who fill your head with demons, devils, and Darwinian predators, far more discombobulating and frightening—especially if you're coming at it from spiritual cold turkey, which almost all of us do.

Now, if the awareness had been nurtured in you, if you had *stayed awake* instead of falling into a spiritual slumber, it wouldn't be this way. But it is and so there you have it. But again, this shouldn't stop you. Like I said, at one time, you were a fish swimming in the water and although we wouldn't want to just throw you back in unprepared, with a little good advice, and a little time to orient and prepare, it doesn't take long for you to get your swim fins back.

Which is, of course, why I'm here.

Like I said earlier, I am going to show you how to access the deeper realities (i.e., I am going to show you how to awaken) and, **most importantly**, I am going to show you how to change your vision of the world so you can see the depths safely and without disjuncture. I am going to teach

49

you how to peek beneath the surface without danger and I am going to do it in such a way that the mind associated with your body (i.e., your bodily ego) will not be frightened, shocked, or otherwise discombobulated by the total awesomeness of it all.

It is not a big deal, really.

All it takes is a bit of spiritual deprogramming so that you can see through the fears and nonsense, and a little basic technique so you can navigate The Waters safely. It's not that hard and, more importantly, and at the risk of unnecessary repetition, it is not a question of skill or talent on your part. You don't have to worry about whether or not you are worthy or "graced" or ready or "initiated" or special or chosen or anything like that. Remember, you are, even now, a fish in The Waters of Consciousness. Once you are confident in your own abilities, the barriers that you yourself have erected in response to your socialization and indoctrination, the barriers that keep you away from The Water, will fall away with little or no effort on your part. When that happens, then I will say, "Welcome to my worldview."

Now, as I said at the beginning, this is a chapter on breathing and although I have not said it yet, I'll definitely say it now. In the context of this discussion of the meniscus and the deep waters of consciousness, breathing is the single most important tool that you need to have in your spiritual repertoire if you are going to go poking at the meniscus of this conscious universe.

Breathing is a tool that you cannot ignore.

You must know how to breathe properly.

You must master breathing because breathing, more than anything else, has incredible ability to ground, enliven, enlighten, awaken, and empower. Bottom line is, breathing will help keep your *egoic* consciousness (i.e., your bodily consciousness) safe and secure as it takes its first tentative dips into the depths of consciousness that lie beneath the surface.

Now I know I am making breathing sound impressive, and it is. What is even more outstanding about it is that breathing is not a difficult tool to master. In fact, even as breathing is the most important tool in this book, it is also the easiest tool to use. The trick is, remembering to do it.

So when do you do it?

When do you deep breath?

Well, whenever you are doing any kind of spiritual work whatsoever, i.e., whenever you approach the meniscus of consciousness, whenever you stick your little toe into the deep waters, whenever you are feeling anxious about what's happening, whenever you are feeling unsure, frightened, or otherwise agitated by "things" around you (spiritual or otherwise), simply engage in a few moments of deep breathing, the deeper and slower, the better.

Allow me to demonstrate.

Do it with me now.

Close your eyes and take ten <u>very</u> deep breaths. *Breathe in* until you cannot breathe in any more, hold for a moment and then exhale, calmly, gently, and with control. <u>Do not force</u> the air into your lungs. Simply fill them to their expanding capacity.

Expand them, stretch them to the limit, and exhale.

Ready?

Breathe in… and exhale…

Breathe in… and exhale…

Put the book down now, close your eyes, focus, and do it eight more times with me.

Go.

…

Done?

Then welcome back.

Now pause for a moment and pay attention to the state of your consciousness as you exit from the deep breathing exercise.

Do you notice the shift?

At the very minimum, when you deep breathe like that you will notice several things. Assuming you are not brutally exhausted and at the end of a long day, you will notice that, as a result of the extra oxygen going to your brain, your "mental alertness" will have increased.

You will also find yourself more focused and more "tuned in."

You will also notice a subtle (and sometimes not so subtle) shift in consciousness.

What kind of shift?

It depends.

It is different for different people.

The truth is, how you experience *the shift*[15] will depend on what you are shifting out of (or into). For example, if before your ten breaths you were feeling anxiety, afterwards you will have shifted and there will be less anxiety. If before breathing you were feeling buzzy and ungrounded, afterwards you will have shifted and be more grounded and calm. If before you were lacking presence in the moment, after you will find yourself more in the "here and now." If before you were experiencing fear, afterwards you will have calmed. In truth, the shift depends on you. However, more importantly than that, you must realize, you control the direction of the shift. If you need to ground yourself, just say as you breathe "I want to be more grounded." If you want calm, say that. Breathe deep and say, "I wish to calm down." Whatever you need to do, intend it and breathe.

_____

[15] Be it a big shift or a small shift, your first shift or the final great shift...

It works!

That's all there is to it.

Now, I cannot overestimate the importance of breathing. As you progress in your awakening process in the days and weeks ahead, breathing will be an important exercise for you, so practice it.

It works.

It is physiological.

It is primordial.

It is deep magic.

Really!

The magic is programmed into the core reality of your body and mind, so learn to do it. And don't let the simplicity of the exercise fool you. It's simple, but it's powerful. No matter how prosaic I might become, I cannot overestimate the importance of breathing. The high truth is this: Breathing is primordial. Breathing is archetypal. Breathing is divine. If you want to get right down to it, breathing is the first act of creation. Breathing is what the original monadic consciousness, the original spark of Light, the

Divine Logos (god with a little "g" if you must know)[16] did upon deciding to create. Breathing was **the first act,** and as such it is a thing that reverberates and is reflected at every layer of reality, in every universe, and at every stage of *The Unfolding*, throughout all of creation.

My god.

Breathing is "the word" of God.

It is powerful beyond measure.

Breathe deep and say to yourself, "I wish clarity," and you will have it.

Breathe deep and say to yourself, "I want to awaken," and the universe will take note and begin moving the energies in order to fulfill.

Know that breathing is the single most calming, grounding, **_life-affirming,_** manifestation-supporting exercise that you can do. When you are feeling anxious, when you are under stress, when you feel threatened, when anxiety wells up, when fear rises up in you, when you want to change direction, when you want to manifest something new, deep breathing helps.

Take breathing seriously.

---

[16] See my *Book of Light: The Nature of God, the Structure of Consciousness, and the Universe Within You* for a definition of god with a little "g" and God with a big "G."

Really, when you think about it, breathing is more important than even food and water for the continuation of your healthy life. You can go weeks without food, days without water, but only seconds without air.

Learn to deep breathe and make it a daily habit.

The practice is powerful beyond measure.

SELF CONFIDENCE AND TRUST

When you are a Bear of Very Little Brain, and you Think of Things, you sometimes find that a Thing which seemed very Thingish inside you is quite different when it gets out into the open and has other people looking at it.

-Winnie the Pooh

In the last section of this spiritual primer I spoke at some length about the importance of deep breathing. As I said there, breathing is important to the grounding process (i.e., it helps keep your consciousness firmly in the 3-D world), it can help with energy generation, and it encourages subtle and positive shifts in consciousness. **Don't forget the lessons on breathing**. Good breathing practice is important at all levels of spiritual awakening and empowerment and is something you should practice on a daily basis.

Now, once you have deep breathing and grounding under control, and once you have practiced and built it into a daily routine, the next step in the process of opening up to the *higher* realities is to learn to trust.

More specifically, the next step is to learn to trust in the spirit world and the consciousness behind creation.

Even more specifically, the next step is to learn to trust God. The bottom line is, if you are going to make any forward progress at all, you are going to have to be able to trust in God, Spirit, your spiritual guide network, the efficacy of the spiritual realm, and the general love that is behind and beneath all manifested creation. Not only this, you are also going to have to trust in your ability to control "things" as you begin to navigate the spiritual halls of consciousness. Trust that God is love, trust that Spirit doesn't wish anything bad to happen to you, and trust that you have the ability to find your way through to "the other side" under your own steam and guidance.

Trusting is _really_ very important.

I can't underline it enough times.

Like the issues of hatred and anger mentioned earlier, if you don't trust, you won't be able to wake up.

Why?

Well, you can understand why if you consider the ugly way that spirituality has been taught to us. As infants, children, teenagers, and even adults, we are all taught to fear and distrust the spirit realm. If we are raised in western religious traditions, we are told awful stories about our failure in The Garden and an abusive, judgmental, and punishing "father" in heaven. We are told stories about demons and devils and hell and purgatory. We are told lies about a violent and hostile spiritual realm. Not only that, we are repeatedly reminded of our insignificance by these traditions. We are told that, in the grander scheme of things, we are less than nothing—throwaway souls fit for annihilation in the fire if we don't "perform" according to the rules. It is a terrible story of our utter spiritual incompetence which, in addition to scaring the bejesus out of our inner child, diminishes us to the point of insignificance and virtual spiritual non-existence. It diminishes us so much that even the idea of confronting our inner divinity terrifies us. We build a thick wall between our waking consciousness and The Waters, and spin circles out of a deep fear of moving forward and confronting our awesome glory.

It's a terrible condition to be in especially as we approach 2012 because as we approach 2012, the wall that you have built up to protect your fragile sensibilities, and to avoid activating the deep fears implanted by the dogmatic systems of this earth, is going to be torn down bit by bit. As the "walls come tumbling down,[17]" and as "The Veil" crumbles, you are going to be forced to confront not only the truth about yourself, but also the awesome reality that is the consciousness of your glorious Spirit. It is going to be a surprise especially if you haven't prepared, because if you haven't, when you meet up with The Waters, all the demons, devils, ghosts, and googly-men that have been put into your head by the priests, pundits, and peanut heads of this world are going to bubble up to greet you and you will experience them as if they are real. When that happens, you are going to have to trust. You are going to have to

---

[17] Cue John Cougar Mellencamp.

remember that what you see is mere illusion, figments created by your powerful spiritual consciousness. Imaginary, yes, but potentially terrifying, I admit. Dragons put there to keep you far away from the meniscus and firmly fetal on the "outside" of The Waters of Creation.

Obviously, that's not where you want to be.

You want to get "to the other side"

So trust.

That's the key.

Trust in the love of God, trust in the magnanimous character of Spirit, and trust that the universe isn't out to get you. It's easy. All you have to do is overcome decades (and multiple lifetimes) of indoctrination. But you'll do it! You'll be fine. And if you fail the first time, don't worry. Just try again.[18] There's no real time limit here. As long as you're working on it, you'll be fine. You have got all the time in the world.

Now, for those of you who consider yourself *outside* of the influence of traditional religious dogma, don't think you're off the hook. Just because you weren't raised in such a background, just because you renounced the twisted beliefs at an early age, doesn't mean you are immune from the dogma or fear. Not only may the fears have been

---

[18] Fall down five times, get up six.

stored deep inside your mind while you were pre-verbal (and therefore they exist even though you are now unaware), or in another lifetime (deep inside your genetic code), there are other sources of fear that have nothing to do with religious sentiment. The truth is, scientists and others of a more rational persuasion can just as easily be terrified of The Waters of Consciousness as any fundamentalist Christian ever was.

The truth is, as born and/or bred atheists, we are also taught to mistrust and even fear the spiritual worlds.

The truth is, as atheists, we are taught to be judgmental and dismissive towards spiritual experience.

As atheists, we are told that the spiritual world is for children, for animists, for primitives, for schizophrenics.

As atheists, we are told that the rational people, the smart people, the "above the curve" people have no use for primitive animisms or pantheistic spiritualities. These are relics of our bygone days as superstitious hunter/gatherers, we are told.

As atheists we are told that spiritual sentiment is a sign of a weakness that should be dominated and suppressed, overcome and controlled by the rational mind.

We must rise above, we are told.

Of course, after hearing all these things from our parents, professor priests, and colleagues, we either turn our back on spirituality altogether, telling ourselves that we are "better" than all that, or we maintain a professionally safe "academic" interest. We keep *The Fabric of Consciousness*, the water beneath the meniscus, at arm's length. If we consider spirituality at all, it is only on the surface. We objectify it, poke it, prod it, observe others experiencing it, but never really get very close to it ourselves. After all, what would our colleagues think?

The fear is different, you see, but the result is the same— fear and avoidance.

Now of course, these are only two examples "at the extreme." Raw religious fears and deep scientific prejudices are only the opposite sides of a continuum of spiritual anxiety that causes us to build a wall between our little ego, our little "I," and the much bigger "I" that exists on the other side of the meniscus. There are other ways that we can be taught to fear the spirit world. In fact, there are many combinations of beliefs and many subtle ways to diminish you in all the spiritual systems of this world. The sorry state of things is, no extant belief system is immune.[19]

Now, if the thought of this makes your head spin, don't worry. Thankfully, we do not have to rehearse all the errors. We can just forget them. Ignore them! Like I said

---

[19] Except this one. I spend a lot of time and energy making sure my teachings are not darkened by the fears, prejudices, and intentional corruptions common in our world belief systems. With me you get the light, the full light, and nothing but the Light—so help me God.

earlier, no matter what your fears are, it's relatively easy to traverse to the other side despite the darkness heaped on the confusion piled high on the misdirection.

All you have to do is trust.

The key is trust.

If you can trust, you'll be fine.

If you can trust, you'll skip right through.

Trust, trust, trust.

Trust is the key.

Unfortunately, besides this admonishment to trust, and the reminder to breathe deep and visualize what you really want, there isn't much I can do to prepare you. When the time comes, it is a simple choice that you will make. You will either trust and move forward or cave to your fear and move back.

Simple.

Just remember, whatever happens, **don't kick your self**!!

If you fail the first time (or the tenth time even), it's <u>no</u> big deal!

Everybody falls. It's nothing to be ashamed off!

If you fail, simply try again. Take as long as you want to compose yourself, and simply try again. Keep at it and one day soon the truth is going to smack you in the forehead like yesterday's raw fish and you'll realize that you are the one manifesting the situations that trigger your fear. When you realize that, *the scale* will tip and you'll be through. As long as you don't give up, your day will come. Until then, don't worry yourself about it.

Have some fun.

Take some playtime.

You will get through.

I promise you.

Just remember your spiritual practice! When you do come to the point where you have to confront your demons, whatever they may be, remember to breathe.

Inhale,

Exhale,

Be calm,

Trust.

Remember!

In this Great Awakening process that you are now undergoing, there is nothing to fear.

Remember!

You are like a fish in the water, so trust.

Frankly, it is good advice wherever you happen to be on your own path of awakening. Even if you don't think you have these big dogmatic fears that I've talked about, it is worthwhile cultivating trust. After all, we are still at the start of the process. We're still rubbing the sleep from our eyes. As a species, we haven't even begun to fully open. By the time we are finished, by the time you are finished this Great Awakening process, you are going to have an entirely new perspective on just about everything you've ever known. You'll be saying goodbye to a millennia of nonsense and saying hello to a glorious new vision of reality and self that does not include space for hierarchy, division, hatred, fear, or diminishment. The intellectual, emotional, and spiritual shift will be huge so even without the big dogmatic fears, chances are that at some point you're going to be asked to take some pretty big leaps. When the time comes, when you face that chasm of credulity, if you want to keep moving forward and not get "turned back," the key will be trust.

Trust me.

This path you're on, this path of global awakening, this path of personal spiritual empowerment, leads not to damnation or madness but to total spiritual awakening and a personal and collective transformation unlike anything the world has ever seen.

It's a good thing that we're doing here.

We're leaving behind the old, ugly world and creating a new one. There's nothing to fear. Embrace the awakening.

Trust is the key.

IGNITION

Did you ever stop to think, and
forget to start again?
~ Winnie the Pooh

So far in this book we have talked about trust, breathing and right thinking. These are the proper foundations for your awakening. Once you have practiced these things for a bit, and they have become a habitual thing, then it's time to consider "starting the engines."

Thankfully, like all things spiritual, starting the engines on your physical body is not that hard. In fact, when you're ready, when you're trusting and breathing, when you're thinking nice thoughts about everything and are at peace with an emerging new vision of reality that doesn't include all the hierarchy and rejection, poverty and suffering, war and chaos of the old way of thinking, then "starting the engines" is quite easy. When you're ready, and, of course, only you know when you're ready, all you have to do to get yourself rolling on The *Lightning Path* is *set your intent*. All you have to do is simply "decide" that you want to awaken. Then, when you have decided, *will it* to happen.

Willfully draw yourself up.

Willfully awaken.

It's easy, and contrary to what you might have been told, it is not a mystical process.

Simply intend and make it so.

What else is there to say about it?

Just do it.

Do it like you do it every morning. Drag your tired body out of bed and drag your consciousness back into your body. It is totally within your power and capability.

Say to yourself (often and with conviction), "I wish to wake into full consciousness as fast and as safely as possible." Then, when you have vocalized your intent, simply stretch, yawn, rub your eyes, and struggle your way up to full consciousness—just like you do every morning.

That's all there is to it.

It is not hard.

It is not rocket science.

It doesn't require a convoluted thesis and it is <u>very</u> effective.

Simply intend yourself awake.

Simply say, "I wish to wake up."

Now, I know it might sound crazy to you right now.

I know it might sound like hocus pocus nonsense, but it's not. Intent, otherwise known as will, is a critical component of everything you do. From getting up in the morning, to cooking breakfast, to going to work, to loving your kids, INTENT is key. When you think about it, the only thing you don't need INTENT for is dying. Dying is the only thing that happens without will. For everything else, intent is important. In fact, it's so important, so basic, that you'll find that this "intent" thing works amazingly well, especially with something as easy and well practiced as waking up to your full consciousness. A little bit of intent, a little bit of effort, some good guidance, and there you go.

It is totally within your power and capability to do.

So intend, intend, intend.

Say, "<u>I will to move forward</u>" and don't take no for an answer. Don't give in to fear, don't give into any ideas about your own insignificance or unworthiness, don't listen to anything about your "sin" or your icky karmic debt, and don't be fooled by scientific prejudice. The deep Waters of Consciousness are real. They lie just beneath the surface of your "normal" reality. So, breath, trust, think nice thoughts, and intend yourself awake.

Repeat after me with conviction, "I wish to wake up."

"I'm ready to wake up."

"I wish to wake up."

Keep an open mind and keep any fear you may have controlled.

Breathe and embrace the morning.

Follow the advice in Part One of this book and you'll be surprised just how fast you'll find yourself waking up.

It really will be a glorious personal transformation and empowerment—a truly great awakening!

It's true.

You'll see.

PART TWO:
ON THE ROADS OF CREATION

STEERING

It is more fun to talk with someone
who doesn't use long, difficult words
but rather short, easy words like
"What about lunch?"
~ Winnie the Pooh

In part one of this book I discussed several concepts and techniques important for your own spiritual awakening process. I discussed right thinking, breathing, intent, and trust. These are all concepts and techniques that you need if you are going to be able to initiate and navigate your own awakening process.

In part two of this book I would like to move beyond the basic "get in your car and start the engine" advice of the previous section and talk more about how to actually steer your vehicle (i.e., your body) and drive it safely through the energetic roadways of creation. Once again, and as I am fond of repeating, the advice and technique provided here isn't hard. It is all pretty basic stuff and you should find that once you get going, once you start your practice, things will fall into place pretty quickly.

Now, we'll start off our "driving advice" in this chapter by taking a look at the body's primary steering mechanism: visualization. In this chapter you will learn about the power and importance of this simple, yet effective, tool for directing the flow of your life. Of course, we won't stop with visualization. After we finish our discussion in this chapter we will move on to discuss things like road safety, how to communicate with other drivers, how to properly maintain the energetic balance of your physical vehicle, and how to properly feed, water, and heal to keep the vehicle running at top efficiency. However, we begin with visualization.

So what is visualization (a.k.a. imagination)?

Well, visualization is basically the ability to "see things" in your brain.

Visualization is the ability to draw a picture in your mind's eye.

That's all there is to it.

If you can *imagine* something in your brain, with your eyes closed if necessary, you are visualizing.

Simple.

However, as with breathing, don't let the simplicity fool you. Like breathing, visualization is a powerful tool. In fact, in terms of your ability to awaken, empower, and steer your way through life, visualization is critical. I can tell you right now, in terms of awakening and driving around the roadways of creation, you won't get very far very fast if you don't learn visualization.

Visualization is a fundamental technique.

It is quite literally the "steering wheel" of your physical vehicle.

To be blunt, visualization is what controls what exists in the world you experience.

Important stuff!

So important, in fact, that it should be taught in grade school.

Sadly, however, it's not.

In fact, past maybe grade two, visualization-friendly activities like painting are actively discouraged in favor of more "practical" skills.[20] However, despite this fact, and as more and more people are beginning to recognize, we should definitely learn. Visualization is a powerful way to direct your life and if you don't learn to visualize, then you *give up* the best opportunity you have to control the world you experience. What's more, if you don't visualize, then (as we shall see in more detail next chapter) you are pretty much at the mercy of whatever other *visions* of reality happen to be operating in your area. Frankly, given some of the ugly visions of reality that are operating these days, leaving yourself open to somebody else's visualization of reality could be hazardous to your health. And it really doesn't matter whose vision of reality it might be. It could be your neighbor, your local politician, some Rothschild sitting in a brown room somewhere, the pope, the president, or even your mom and dad. As I noted in Part

---

[20] I explore education and pedagogical issues in the online forums at www.michaelsharp.org

73

One, there are a lot of weird ideas about the way creation works, and you just never know what people "have in mind" (either consciously or unconsciously) for you.

Word to the wise: steer your own course and manifest your own world by using the basic spiritual techniques, like visualization, provided here.

Now, perhaps at this point you are asking "Why does visualization work and how do I do it?" As to why, I'll explain in more detail about the technical aspects of visualization in subsequent books.[21] For now, the sound bite explanation will have to do and here it is. Energy is really just a "stepped down" form of consciousness and as such, energy responds in a direct and literal fashion to the contents of your consciousness.

As above in consciousness, so below in matter.

Bottom line, if you think about something, then the "energy" that makes up the universe begins to move *in the direction* of your thinking. Keep something in your mind long enough and the energy of creation will eventually manifest your vision.

This is *the* basic principle of creation.

Whatever is in your brain determines the universe that you experience.

_____

[21] Particularly in *The Book of Light* and *The Book of Magic*.

Whatever you dream in your soul (above) manifests in creation (below).

More or less, anyway.

Truth is, on this earth it's not always so easy and straightforward. On this earth, there is always a lot of interference from, for example, sleepyheads who think it's okay to actively impose their horrible visions of life, the universe, and everything on others. Under these *creatively hostile* conditions, even if you have a very clear visualization of what you want (which most of you don't yet), and even if you have total confidence in that vision (doubtful, considering the spiritually hostile conditions we live under), you can't always manifest what you want as fast as you want because of all the interference. Still, you shouldn't let the difficulty stop you. I'm not saying this to discourage you but to encourage you to take control. Until conditions aren't so "hostile" to your heart's desire, you'll simply need to have patience and persistence in order to steer the vehicle and create the world you want. You don't do yourself any favors by backing out of this potential because it's a little difficult, and besides, creative conditions on this earth won't be hostile forever. Times are a changing as we speak and by 2012, you'll find a lot less resistance to the visions in your head.[22]

---

[22] We can only hope, for the sake of the children of this planet, that by 2012, most of us have replaced the "ugly visions" of the world with nicer visions, like the ones suggested in this **free** Book.

It might be frustrating at first, but learning to visualize, learning to steer, will definitely be worth your while both in the short term and the long term. It will be beneficial not only in terms of being able to control the world around you and manifest your desire, **it is also be critical for your spiritual awakening process!** I'm not exaggerating when I say that visualization, like breathing and trust, is one of the keys of rapid and safe spiritual awakening.

But wait a minute.

How does that work?

Didn't I just say, "as above in consciousness, so below in matter?"

Haven't I been saying that visualization is all about the physical world?

Well, yes, I did and, yes, it is.

However, pause for a moment and consider.

Breathe.

Remember this truth:

Your body...

Your brain...

Your nervous system...

Your mind...

Your heart, your voice, your muscles, your arms, your legs, and the blood that flows in your veins are **all made up of physical matter.**

Do you see?

Your physical vehicle, your body, is made up of the energy of creation. Therefore, your body, nervous system, and brain respond to visualization **just like every other physical thing in the universe does**. Therefore, treat your body/mind like the physical object that it is. If you want your body to be healthy,[23] visualize a healthy body (and don't forget to eat right and exercise!). If you want your mind to awaken, visualize an awakening mind.

Simple.

Control your physical body and physical mind through visualization just as you would control any other aspect of the physical universe.[24]

Breathing, intent, and visualization!

That's all there is to it.

---

[23] Especially in this toxic post-industrial soup we call modern city life.

[24] If you want, I have a meditation called *The Great Invocation* that provides a powerful and simple awakening and empowerment visualization. The meditation is included in my book *Dossier of the Ascension: A Practical Guide to Chakra Activation and Kundalini Awakening* and is also available for free on my website. www.michaelsharp.org

Now, as great as this basic technique of visualization is (especially when coupled with breathing and intent), there is one problem that we have to surmount before we can efficiently make use of the power of visualization. The problem is simple. As a result of what I can only call the "slave training" we get in schools, many of us have lost our ability to visualize. That is, as a result of what we all mistakenly called "education," our "right brain" capabilities, our visual, metaphoric, and imaginary powers have atrophied, through no fault of our own, to the point of failure. This makes visualization a problem for a lot of us.

That's okay, though.

It's not that big a deal.

It's not like we are permanently damaged.

We can regain our ability to visualize any time we want and we can strengthen it to whatever level we desire by engaging in some simple right brain activities.

It is easy and you should start immediately.

There are lots of ways you can do it and I'm going to list only a few. Use your imagination to come up with other ways and trust your own intuition about what kind of practice might work for you.

And whatever you do, don't rush it.

Be patient.

The ability to visualize will come back to you. I promise you.

So here is what you do:

Pick up a musical instrument and find a good teacher.

Hang out with children.

Study art.

Try creative writing.

Go take dancing lessons.

Do something kinesthetic.

Do something artistic.

Do something creative.

Make a pot, paint a picture, write a song and don't let me hear you whining, "But I don't have any talent" or "I'm not good at anything."

It is not true.

Talent is <u>not</u> god-given.

Talent is merely the crystallized effect of extended practice.

The truth is, Mozart, Beethoven, Galileo, Picasso or any of the other super talented individuals in this world loved doing "their thing" so much that they were willing to devote *lifetimes* to it. That's why they appear talented. Not because god gave them a "gift," but because they have had, out of sheer love of their art, divine-like commitment to their craft. You too can learn to play piano and compose like Mozart if you spend a dozen lifetimes learning music as he did. Of course, most of us don't have that kind of commitment and that's okay. You don't need that kind of commitment and talent to visualize properly. You just need to get your right brain energies moving again.

You just need to do a little practice.

So, get some right brain practice and, while you're at it, practice your ability to visualize. Picture what it is you want in your mind. If you have difficulty, if you can't do it initially, try again. Start simple by visualizing energy flows. Visualize colors in the air, energy pipes in your room, or chakra activations if you feel so inclined. Then, move to simple geometrics (i.e., boxes and stuff). If you have trouble with that, find a real box (like a jewelry box or something), look at it, close your eyes and try to see it in your mind's eye. When you look at the box and close your eyes, you should find that the image lingers, even if only briefly. When the image fades, do it again, and again, and again until your ability to visualize builds up. Consider this an exercise and practice it often with boxes, flowers, pens, or with anything you happen to have to hand. If you have initial difficulty, stick at it. Keep up with the right brain activities (music, art, etc.), keep practicing the visualization, and eventually your mind's ability to visualize and imagine will come back to you. As it does, don't be afraid![25] Joyfully

---

[25] If you do find yourself getting "scary" images and thoughts, just push them away. Get rid of them. **Don't dwell on them!** If you dwell on them you'll be giving them more and more reality, so

embrace it. It is the joy that you add to the process that will speed your awakening along at light speed.

As a final practical technique, you may also want to try having an internal dialogue with yourself. That is, talk to yourself. Talking to your self is a great way to enhance right brain activity. All children do it. Indeed, many children go so far as to have imaginary friends. Of course, as adults we find this creative ability beaten out of us. The attack on your wise, intuitive, spiritually connected right hemisphere starts with gusto around the age of eight and culminates in the total imaginary vacuum of the "normal" adult. Still, it's like riding a bike. Just because it's forgotten doesn't mean it's gone. Take steps to recapture the imaginative innocence of childhood. It will pay off in your life in ways that you cannot yet imagine.

One final comment: if it takes you a while to get this right, don't worry. Recapturing your full ability to visualize is not a requirement of awakening. Breathing is critical, trust is critical, but visualization is not. As long as you breathe correctly and can summon trust, you will be carried along in the rising tide of the Great Awakening as it occurs on this planet. Truth is, nobody can stay asleep much longer, so you are going to wake up no matter whether you learn to visualize or not. However, you will find the process easier

---

just push them away. I recommend you give those nasty thoughts and dark images a good swift and solid kick in the behind as you shove them, with due haste, out the front door. Don't argue with them. Get rid of them as soon as they pop up. That's the way.

and more pleasant, and you won't have to wait for "the tide," if you take firm control early on and visualize exactly how you want your awakening (and the awakening of those around you) to happen. If you want help with your own practice, I have an awakening visualization called *The Great Invocation*. This activation and awakening meditation is available for free on my website at www.michaelsharp.org and is also provided in my book *Dossier of the Ascension: A Practical Guide to Chakra Activation and Kundalini Awakening.*

Trust, intend, and imagine!

Start now.

Practice often.

> *As above in consciousness, so below in matter.*

The future of your life, and the future of this world, is contained in the images and ideas in your brain. Take control of those images and ideas and create a better world for yourself and everyone else.

Trust yourself.

Breathe and manifest.

You have the power and wisdom within you to steer your own course through life.

ROAD SAFETY

*Don't underestimate the value of
Doing Nothing, of just going along,
listening to all the things you can't
hear, and not bothering*
~ Winnie the Pooh

In the last chapter we talked about the importance of visualization. There you learned that visualization is quite literally the "steering wheel" that your Immortal Spirit uses to steer through the roadways of creation and manifest the life you live. It is not an exaggeration to say that, all other things being equal, visualization has the potential to determine the things that manifest in your life and the direction your life is going. If you want something to happen, or not to happen for that matter, then put a nice detailed visualization of it in your head and intend that thing to happen. When you do, the energy of the universe begins to flow into the vision you have in your head and the work of manifesting that vision begins. [26]

---

[26] As you can see, nothing difficult or mystically complicated about this process! Really, this is magical "grade school" stuff that should be taught to all of us as part of our school curriculum. One day, very soon, it will be.

In this chapter, I want to move beyond breathing, intent (i.e., the things that get your car/body started), and visualization (steering) to talk more about what you have to do to stay "safe on the road."

It is an important topic.

Spiritual "road safety" is important for pretty much exactly the same reasons that regular road safety is important. When you get behind the wheel of that 3-D vehicle of yours (i.e. your car), **you have to remember**, you're not the only driver on the road. When you drive your car you have to drive responsibly. You have to avoid "bumping into things" and you have to drive defensively to prevent others (who may not be paying attention, may be sleeping at the wheel, may be drunk, or otherwise operating with diminished capacity) from bumping into you and causing you bodily harm.

It's the same way when you get into your body/vehicle. When your consciousness "steps into" the body/vehicle, fires it up, and gets it rolling, you have to try to avoid the bumps. Not only that, **you have to remember** you're not the only one on the road. Not only do you have to **drive safely** to ensure you're not hurting others but, because you never can tell the "state of consciousness" of the other drivers on the road with you, you have to **drive defensively** to avoid any bumps from others who may be still "sleeping at the wheel."

So how do you do that? How do you drive safely and defensively while your Spirit is driving around in your physical body?

Well, as with all things spiritual, it involves *ideas*. Remember the "sacred principle" I introduced earlier, *as above in consciousness, so below in matter*. Remember, we use this principle to remind ourselves that what we think affects the world around us, including our bodies.

It's an important spiritual principle to remember.

Energy follows thought.

Visualize something, and the energies move to make it so.

Now, we already know to visualize and intend in order to move our individual vehicle around, but now, as we fire up our vehicles, and later, as we turbo charge them,[27] we need to also understand that the ideas that we have in our head, the visions that we have in our mind and that we use to direct our vehicle through life, affects the *world of others* as well. "No man [sic] is an island," as John Donne said. If you have negative thoughts about your neighbors, for example, or if you go around wishing that your enemies get hurt, you are giving energy to the manifestation of these ideas and increasing the probability of their occurrence. The truth is, if you give enough energy to these ideas, and there are no counteracting influences, they'll eventually happen. In effect, you are using your soul's physical vehicle to bump others around on the road.

----

[27] See my *Dossier of the Ascension: A Practical Guide to Chakra Activation and Kundalini Awakening.*

Now, you shouldn't do that.

Bumping others around with the thoughts in your head isn't good road etiquette. It's not "safe driving" so if you're doing it, stop.

It's easy.

If you want to stop bumping others around on the road, just stop thinking bad thoughts about them. That's all. You don't have to go around loving everybody if you don't want to. No flower power, granola eating necessary here.[28] It is okay to not like someone; but, if you don't like them, don't think about them. Just push them out of your consciousness and don't consider them. That is all you have to do. If you do that, you'll be following good spiritual road etiquette and you will avoid mucking up the driving experience of others.[29]

Now, of course, driving is always a two way street. There's always others on the road with you. A good driver recognizes this fact, takes it into account and drives

---

[28] Although personally, I love flowers and granola.

[29] Avoiding mucking up other's driving experiences is a good thing. If you muck up another's driving experience, you owe them in a "karmic" sense for that interference. You'll have to "make it up to them" at some point. If you do a lot of mucking around, you'll have a lot to make up for and that can keep you busy at The Wheel longer than you might want to be. If you want my advice, stop bumping others around so you can stop accumulating those annoying "responsibility" points and get on with the task of awakening and empowering your body and mind.

defensively. I mean, you can never tell the "state" of the drivers around you right? It would be great if the other people on the road would follow good road etiquette, drive safely, and not muck around with your driving experience. But you just never know. Unfortunately, while most of the people on this earth stay sleeping, you can't really trust others to be polite drivers. For one thing, most people still don't have a clue about *as above in consciousness, so below in matter* and so wouldn't think twice about having (sometimes extremely) negative thoughts about you. For another, your friends, your family, your co-workers, your colleagues, and even your older kids can really put a monkey wrench in your driving plans when they are not thinking and controlling their own negativity. You can't blame them. They don't know better. However, at the same time, you want to stay mostly out of their way to avoid any unfortunate bumps or crashes.

And you know, it is not just the people who you normally drive around with that you have to worry about. People on the opposite side of the world can have ideas about you that have a profound impact on your driving experience as well. This works at the personal, national, and international levels. I certainly wouldn't want to be living in a nation that everyone else is coming to hate and fear. You just know that in conditions like that, and according to the principle *as above in consciousness, so below in matter,* sooner rather than later all that negativity is going to lead to a bump or two.

And you know, it's not just the people you drive around with, and the people who don't like you, that you have to worry about. You also have to consider that some people out there have weird ideas about how the world works. As you know, there are people out there who actually believe in evil, for example. There are people who believe in sin. There are even people who believe in divinely sanctioned hierarchy, poverty, and war. Heck, there's people who think that during the "end times," God is going to come flashing down in order to rain fiery death and destruction on the "unworthy" of this earth.

I know...

It's absurd, but people believe it anyway.

In fact, many people believe.

Indeed, enough people on this earth currently believe in that nonsense to manifest it (as above in consciousness, so below in matter). Now, I don't know about you, but I don't want to be on the same road as them when they manifest that nonsense. In fact, I want my family and I to avoid that energy altogether. Frankly, I don't want to have anything to do with it and, good news, I don't have to.

The truth is, I can totally avoid that stuff if I want to.

I can avoid the negativity of my friends and family who don't know better, the hatred of my enemies who are "out to get me" (even if only in their thoughts), and even the crazy ideas people have about the way the universe works if I just build a little white energy barrier around my life.

It is very easy to do.

Here's how.

To do it, to block out the little black energetic "slings and arrows" that people send at you inadvertently with their gray and black thought patterns, simply visualize a white ball of energy, a halo of light, surrounding your body about five inches away from your skin. *Keep in mind the following ideas while you do it.* This halo that you create by visualizing is an impenetrable energetic barrier of light. Its purpose is to allow positive and life affirming energies in, but to keep all negative energies (no matter where they come from) away from your creative spaces, thereby protecting the integrity of your these spaces. The barrier is impenetrable to all negativity. Nothing that is harmful to you or the ones you love gets in. Everything energy that is supporting to you and uplifting of your creative spaces, passes through unhindered.

This is all there is to it.

Visualization and intent.

Now, considering how many people there are out there with weird ideas and negative thought patterns, it is wise to spend some time each day building up and strengthening your barrier. There are a couple things you can do to do that. For one thing, you can strengthen the protective action of the barrier by visualizing the protective action of the barrier. Simply see little black energy streams, like little black thought arrows, bouncing of the barrier of light without any effect. Don't stop there either. Visualize the opposite action as well. Visualize little white thought arrows (positive and supportive thoughts and energies) penetrating the barrier in order to strengthen the reality you choose to manifest. It's that easy. Combine these two visualization strategies into an effective and powerful safety mechanism. You'll be amazed at the results.

Another way to strengthen the action of the barrier is to actually build the barrier up. To do that, simply take a deep breath and, as you exhale, see little sparkling white energy nodules floating around your body and entering into your halo. Breathe in and draw the infinite, whisperous tendrils of white energy that surround your body into the halo that you create. As the energy enters, see how the halo strengthens. As you add energy, the halo goes from a pale and translucent white to a thick and solid barrier of energy. Keep building this barrier up by adding energy to it over a few days or weeks and when you are satisfied it is strong enough to protect you, then begin to expand it away from your body to include your close family, your house, your car, your work, and anything else that you want to preserve and keep safe from the weird ideas and negativity of others. Go as far as you want with this. Expand this barrier in the days and weeks ahead as wide and as thick as you care to. Keep in mind that there is no limit on how strong the barrier can be. However, if you want my advice, given current conditions of this world, the stronger you make that barrier, the better.

Building up the barrier and keeping those negative and crazy ideas out will be beneficial for you. It will pay off in the short and long term in ways that may surprise you. For example, you'll find that once you deny the negativity of others into your space, you'll make better progress in anything you happen to be doing, whether it's spiritual awakening, manifesting a new job, fixing your family relationships, or whatever.

The exercise is worthwhile; and, don't let up on this barrier until either the world is a much better place or you are absolutely certain of the power of your own divinity and therefore absolutely convinced of your immunity from negativity. My advice is, keep this barrier in mind, and teach this ritual to others for at least the next 20 years, maybe a bit more. I figure it will be at least 20 years until enough people have awakened and put aside the crazy ideas and unthinking negativity of their daily round to make it safe to go about in this world "unprotected."

Until that day comes, protect yourself while you are on the road.

Do the visualization daily.

Now I'd like to make one final comment before closing this section off. When you build this barrier, when you build the halo and expand it into a wall that protects your entire life space, you are going to find that "things change" in your life. Relationships especially are going to rearrange themselves in sometimes subtle and sometimes dramatic ways. For example, as you do the protection ritual, you may find that people whom you never would have thought had any negative intent towards you suddenly become "distant." Depending on negotiations at the soul level, and the level of discomfort that these negative influences feel from being around you, they may even bump right out of your life temporarily (while they learn to be less negative or learn to release some of the silly ideas they carry around) or permanently (if they refuse to change).

Don't be surprised when that happens.

I'm telling you now, you may even find that some of your closest friends and family members are suddenly too busy to spend time with you. If that happens, keep in mind the purpose of the protection ritual. Remember, the ritual is designed to give you the space you need in order to manifest the life and the conditions that you want to manifest. In other words, you are doing this for self-preservation and so you can wake up easier and faster, so do not get freaked out by the change. Remember, you initiated the process for your benefit and you have control. If you want, you can always allow these negative people back into your space once you get control of your own awakening process. When you feel comfortable, invite them back in a superficial "Hi, how are ya, how's the weather" sort of way or deeper if you want. However, make a reasoned decision. Never forget that these people are sleeping at the wheel and, because of that, they can be unpredictable and even dangerous. If you are going to go driving around them, for whatever reason, drive with extra caution and protect yourself while on the roads.

Now, if the loss of people in your life bothers you too much, keep in mind that the shifting relationships are not necessarily permanent. Everybody eventually has to wake up so as long as something bad doesn't happen to the sleepy heads while they sleep (accidents, cancer, voluntary exits, things like that), they'll probably come back into your life, only at a deeper and more resonate level, a little later. Be open to that possibility. Don't keep the boundaries so rigid that you permanently exclude, no matter how negative or weird they might have been. In fact, if you want, you can actually help them wake up. Encourage change and awakening in them by visualizing the same process of waking up that you do. I have a meditation designed for this purpose called *The Great Purification.* It is available at my website at www.michaelsharp.org.

A word of warning though.

When it comes to "helping" others awaken, don't push too hard and, more importantly, don't push at all if you can't see what's going on in their life or how they are reacting. It is fine to help others awaken by visualizing forward progress for them, but if you push people in a direction they are not ready to go in, they will resist, sometimes aggressively and violently. The truth is, you can do damage to them or others (like their children, their spouses) if they react aggressively. You want to avoid that that under all circumstances. It is not right when others interfere with your own life plans. It is even less acceptable for someone who is "in the know" to interfere with the life paths of others. The more you *know,* the more you must take care of others.

A final word before closing: If you find yourself in the role of parent or protector of others who are weak, innocent, or in need of defense, stand your ground and keep the barriers strong no matter what. If you are by yourself it may be okay to allow some degree of negativity into your space. You may be able to handle it. You may know what to do. However, you are not doing yourself, your children, or anyone else you are responsible for any favors by allowing the negativity into the life space of those you are responsible for protecting. As a parent, it is your job to protect your children and prevent them from coming to any harm <u>whatsoever</u>.

It's your job.

Take it seriously.

If you're protecting others, especially the special children (i.e., the crystal children) being born these days, no compromise is appropriate. When there are little ones involved, get the negativity away and keep it away, period.

Build the barrier.

Keep it strong.

ROADSIDE COMMUNICATION

People who don't think probably
don't have Brains; rather, they have
gray fluff that's blown into their
heads by mistake.
~ Winnie the Pooh

At this point in this book we have come a long way. We have talked about many important concepts and techniques, all of which are necessary for activation and proper operation of your physical vehicle. We have looked at things like trust, breathing, visualization, intent, and protection rituals. Now, with these things rehearsed and part of our daily practice, it is time to consider opening up a channel of communication.

What kind of communication channel?

Basically, a channel of communication to the spirit world.

Specifically, a channel of communication to your guide network.

What's your guide network?

Well, your guide network is a tight collection of *disincarnate* spiritual entities who are here to "guide" you and assist you and who want nothing more than to hover around and provide you with the energetic and support services you need to complete your chosen work.

That's all.

They are here to help and uplift you.

That's it.

Now, a lot of people have the mistaken idea that your guides are like *teachers* or *directors* whose job is to **direct** you through life and tell you what to do. However, that's not the way it is. Your Spirit guides are not more knowledgeable than you, more spiritual than you, more wise than you, or more "good" than you. Truth be told, you are the one with the knowledge and the experience. You are the one that is *at the front line,* so to speak, and because of that, because you have a direct connection with the material world we are creating, your guides cannot sensibly direct you. It doesn't make any sense. It would be like a landlubber who's never been in a boat trying to tell an experienced sea-faring captain how to pilot the ship—with a cell phone, a thousand miles away, without being able to see what's in front of the ship.

Craziness.

Really, your guides are more like disincarnate friends and family members who offer you advice, energetic assistance and, if you want it, gentle and supportive guidance—but only if you ask. And let me be clear here, if you want your guides to help, you need to ask them. Not only will your guides *never* make a decision for you, they will also *never* do anything to you without your permission.

You are totally in control here.

You are, quite literally, the captain of your ship. As I explain in *The Parable of The Garden* (included in the appendix of this book), your spiritual guides are there to help you "do your job." They are there to help you find your way around in the darkness of this earth and nothing more.

Now, I've got to say that, in all cases, your guides are very good at providing you assistance. If you ask them for advice, chances are they have the answer, and that's not because they are smarter than you, it is just because they know you well. In fact, because your consciousness is "veiled," i.e., because you have been sleep walking on this earth, when you start out, your guides literally know you and the purpose for which you incarnated better than you yourself do. In fact, when it comes to the whys, the wherefores, and the "where am I going" types of questions, your guides have the answer, at least initially.

But remember this.

Your guides aren't babysitters.

They won't be around you forever. They are just there to help you through the first stages of your awakening process. Once you've got it under control, your guides are no longer needed and they will *step back* in order that you can make your own decisions and that's a good thing. It is something to shoot for. You want to get to a point where you are confident enough in your own abilities to pilot without advice. It shouldn't take that long to get there, but until you do, trust your guides. Your guides are there to serve and ensure a safe awakening.

So, question before us now is, how do you contact your guides?

How do you *open a channel* of communication to them?

Well, like all things spiritual, it is very easy. All you have to do to open a channel to your guide network is visualize a connection of some sort. The easiest, and therefore most powerful, visualization that I can think of is to simply visualize an "energy pipe" starting from your brain center and passing through your skull up into the spiritual world.

Simply see a tube exiting your skull. See the pipe as it exits your skull widen and expand into a huge cosmic funnel where energy flows through a narrow "point of contact" into your skull, brain, and Central Nervous System (CNS). Focus in on the energy now and notice how, as it flows, it enlivens your entire nervous system. As the energy enters, your brain lights up, your nerves sparkle with energy, and your body glows with the light-energy flowing in and through you. Now, as you visualize this scene in your head, notice how you can control the flow of energy. You can squeeze the energy flow right off and therefore "cut yourself off" from the funnel that connects you to *The Fabric of Consciousness* (a.k.a. The Waters of Creation), or you can speed up the energy flow and even expand the funnel to encompass the entire universe and beyond.

Keep in mind this next very important point:

There is no limit to how wide that funnel can become and no external control over the process. You turn the spigot on or off. You specify the energy flow and you control how wide or narrow the channel is.

Now, most of you reading these words will have a closed off channel of communication. Don't feel bad. It's not your fault and, as adults, we are like that. We don't start off that way as children. Oh, no! As children we have a wide-open channel to The Fabric. However, for reasons I outline throughout my writings, as we grow into teenagers and adults, we close that channel off.

Why?

Basically, we close it off because we are taught to be afraid of it.

We close it because we are taught that we are tiny and irrelevant.

We close it because we are told it is filled with demons and devils and tricksters of every kind.

We close it because we are told judgment awaits us "on the other side."

We close it off because of all the religious and scientific gobbledy-gook we hear.

It comes down to this: we close it off because we don't want to connect with the "other side." We have been taught deep fear of The Waters of Consciousness and so we put up a wall, build a meniscus, and shut down the connection. We then put on this big show for ourselves and everybody else about how we don't understand and we can't connect and we don't have the power and oh gosh, and oh darn, gee, golly whiz.

Ah, but, dear chela, you do have the power to open. You have total authority over the channel. All you have to do is visualize that pipe and "the channel" is instantly opened.

Simple.

Now, as strange as this might sound to some of you, and although I've given you a lot of tools and advice in this book to prepare you for opening a channel, I wouldn't recommend blasting that skull pipe open just yet. My advice, no matter who you are and what types of communication you may have had in the past, is to start slow. Remember what I have said. The reality on the other side of that pipe is vast and mind boggling and even with the breathing and the intent and the visualization and the safe driving lessons and the protection and all the help from your guides, you still want to proceed with caution. [30]

Open a little bitty pipe at first and allow just a thin sliver of energy to pass back and forth.

-----

[30] In other words, stay away from the magic mushrooms for a while.

Don't overdo it, but do it like you do all the other visualizations you do. Do it for a few seconds whenever you think about it, several times a day, persistently until "things" start happen.

What kind of things?

Well, since it's a tiny connection you open at first, you'll be looking for "meaningful" things to happen.

"Synchronous" things.

You know what synchronicity is, right?

Synchronicity, according to Carl Gustaf Jung, is the occurrence of an extremely unlikely event with *deep personal significance and meaning*. A synchronicity is a remarkable, nay astounding coincidence, but not just any coincidence. A synchronicity is a coincidence of epic proportions. It is an event, a confluence of person, place, and thing that is unmistakably personal, meaningful, and outrageously cosmic in its statistical improbability.

The "event," the synchronicity, could be anything. It could be something your neighbor says, it could be some weird and inexplicable electronic malfunction, it could be a vehicle driving in front of you, it could be a beggar on the street approaching, it could be a number flashing repeatedly before you,[31] or anything under the sun as long

---

[31] 11:11 anyone?

as it has personal meaning and as long as it is so statistically improbable that when you experience it, you just know "something" is going on.

So what's this "synchronicity" have to do with talking to your guides? Well, unless you do something foolish and blast the channel open before you have properly prepared yourself, synchronicity is the first "channel" that your guide network will use to communicate with you. In fact, when you open your skull pipe up just a little itty bit, it's the only one they can use. So if you're coming at this with no previous experience, when you start the "pipe visualization," when you open an itty-bitty bit, pay attention! Your first communications will be in the form of synchronicity.

Now, synchronicity is an okay kind of communication channel to use. The good thing about synchronicity is not only can your guide network actually get a "message" to you without much ambiguity,[32] it keeps a nice safe boundary between your ego and the rest of the Spirit world. This is a good thing, especially if you have some fears about the spirit world that you aren't aware of and that might become activated if you get too close to the meniscus. This way, you can get a communication from Spirit without actually confronting your fears. Thus, it's a good starting point because it allows the sleeping mind of

---

[32] Given the statistical improbability of the synchronicity, it cannot be rationally denied.

the body, the mind that is unfamiliar with the deep realities of Spirit, to *see* that something big is going on without becoming terrified by the implications. Synchronicity is a slow dose of communication meted out in safe measure designed to ensure the integrity of the ego.

Synchronicity happens a lot in your life, a lot more than you realize, especially these days. In fact, it is often the case these days that those in the spirit world who have an interest in you[33] have some kind of "life or death" message to get through to you. Unfortunately, until we actually start to pay attention, we tend to miss a lot of the "desperate" messages our guide network tries to send us because although a synchronous event is easy to see if you're paying attention, because of the subtle nature of the event, it's also easy to miss if you aren't looking.

Also important to note, synchronicity is also something you can control. That is, you don't have to stand around waiting for your guide network to send you a message. Be proactive! Ask a question and wait twenty-four to forty-eight hours for the answer. I recommend a simple question like "are you there" or "who am I" or something like that. Keep an open mind, too. The answer you get, especially to the "who am I" quesstion, may surprise you.

Now, the bad thing about synchronicity it that is has a couple of profound limitations. First of all, although you can

---

[33] For example, your dead family members, your spiritual guides, etc.

always tell that something is "going on" when you catch a synchronous message, that's about all you can tell. Owing to the difficulty of arranging material events in an improbable but meaningful sort of way, the message sent to you is *always* a simple message and *often* merely an empty message—meaning that the only meaning to be found is in the fact that the event is meaningful—and that's okay, at the start, anyway. The point "at the start" isn't to communicate profound spiritual wisdom or to engage in a deep spiritual conversation.[34] The point is to simply start the process of getting you used to the idea that there's "something big" going on beneath the surface. Once you get used to the idea, then it is time to graduate and move on.

A word to the wise here:

Whatever you do, don't get hung up on synchronicity. Synchronicity is okay for what it is, but amongst all the methods of getting a message through the meniscus,

---

[34] Of course, this profound limitation hasn't prevented some people from going all crazy trying to find the "deep," "hidden," "esoteric" meanings behind synchronous events. Unfortunately for the likes of Jung, there usually isn't any deep meaning to the synchronicity. Synchronous events are meaningful for what they are, i.e., highly improbable events that defy explanation within a materialist, dualist framework. In other words, the meaning of the synchronous event is to be found in the event itself and attempts to "pry the depths" is foolhardy. Like my old buddy Sigmund Freud once said from his cocaine induced mental fog, sometimes a cigar is just a cigar.

synchronicity is the most "primitive," most indirect, most difficult form of communication that can happen. It takes your guide network immense concentration and intent to arrange even the simplest events. Therefore, if you "hang on" to synchronicity, you are asking a lot from your guides. I can tell you now, they won't carry on banging their heads against your stubborn refusal to "see" forever. If you don't move on to easier and more effective forms of spiritual communication, they will stop trying. When that happens, you've either got to wait for them to chill out enough to want to try and get a message through your stubborn-ass head again, or you are going to spontaneously move on to an easier (for them) form of communicating. You just can't ask them to keep doing it for you. They'll eventually give up. Trust your own eyes. If the event seems impossible within the rational confines of a materialist universe, it is.

Once you get the message that there is "something going on" beneath the surface of this reality, and presuming you don't get freaked out and fearful, then the next step is to open the skull pipe a little wider. You already know how to do that. To do it, simply visualize the narrow pipe widening a bit. How much? Trust your intuition. A little bit or a lot, it's up to you. Of course, once you decide how much, then you do it like you do all the visualizations you do. Visualize for a few moments, persistently and faithfully, several times a day, until "things" start happen.

What kinds of things?

Well, "feeling" things.

Emotional things.

105

Bodily things.

When you open that skull pipe of yours a little wider, start paying attention to your body.

Why?

Because external spiritual influence on your actual physical body, i.e., spiritual manipulation of the subtle systems of your body, is the next step in opening a full channel to the spiritual world.

Perhaps at this point you are asking yourself, how can a disincarnate spirit influence my physical body? Well, when you are willingly open to the influence, or when you are not aware of your absolute spiritual sovereignty and therefore "open by mistake," it is easy. In fact, the same high spiritual principle that that governs the interaction of consciousness with the physical universe operates here as well.

As above in consciousness,
So below in matter.

Just as *you* control the physical world through the thoughts you have in your head, and just as disincarnated Spirit can communicate with you by influencing the external *material world*, consciousness (whether in a body or not) can influence your body. After all, your body and your mind are part of the material world and, like all aspects of the material world, your body (and mind) respond to consciousness pure and simple. Therefore, communicating with you through your body is a lot easier than communicating through synchronicity. Indeed, All Immortal

Spirit has to do to *communicate* in this fashion is *influence* your body in a way that is noticeable to you. Typically, Spirit targets your CNS in order to provide you with some kind of *sensation*.

What kind of sensation?

Well, that depends on the message. If it's a happy message that everything is okay and you can keep going on your merry way, then you'll have happy sensations. However, if it's an urgent message of a type like "WAKE UP, YOU'RE HEADING FOR A WALL, YOU'RE GOING TO CRASH!" then it's a more urgent sensation. It could be anything. It could be a "worry" feeling meaning something bad is going to happen if you don't do something. It could be bad feelings about yourself meaning you're doing something wrong and getting away from your chosen life's purpose. It could even be pleasant little tingly "resonations" telling you "MONEY," you're right on the mark. It really just depends. So pay attention to your feelings. You never know who might be trying to talk to you.

Now, using your CNS to get a message to you is a great method of communication. In terms of the quality of the message, it's much better than synchronicity. Synchronicity is a blunt hammer compared to the subtle possibilities that open when you enable bodily communication through your CNS. Using your CNS is also safe for the ego, since, if you are still a little frightened by the depths beneath the surface, you can just assume it's your own body acting on its own. You don't have to confront or commit to the idea of the meniscus at all here, at least until you've learned to trust that your emotional senses will guide you accurately through your life path.

Of course, as you would expect, CNS communication has some limitations. Like synchronicity, the kind of message you get with the CNS method of communication is always very simple. In other words, you cannot get a lot of detail through. It is no more than a binary "good feeling/bad feeling" sort of thing. You can manage general advice through this, i.e., advice like, "Turn left," "turn right," "go straight," or "get the hell out of DODGE right now," but that's about the extent of the message you can get. Obviously, because of limitations of CNS communication, you don't want to rely on this form of channel for very long, although you can if you want to. Unlike synchronicity, your guide network doesn't find it tiresome to communicate through your CNS system. In fact, if you are stubborn, it can go on for decades. Still, you don't want it to. As with synchronicity, don't get hung up on feelings. Once you're comfortable with the notion that other beings can influence your body, once the idea that the boundary between you and "everything else" isn't a solid wall like you were raised to think it was, and once you're convinced that this is okay and nothing bad is going to happen to you because of it,[35] move on and expand the pipe a bit more. Do it almost exactly like you did it the last time, only this

---

[35] That is, you don't believe in silly things like demonic possession, madness, or things like that.

108

time extend the energies down through your brain and also out the middle of your forehead.

In fact, do the funnel thing again.

Visualize a funnel sticking out of the top of your head and a funnel sticking out of the spot just above and between your eyes. Visualize these two pipes as wide or as narrow as you want. Trust your intuition as to how wide and how much energy will flow. When you get a good idea, start the visualization. Do it like you do all the visualizations. Do it for a few moments whenever you think about it, several times a day. Be persistent and do it every day until "things" start happen.

What kinds of things?

Well, "intuition types of things."

"Sixth sense" types of things.

Even idea and image types of things.

I mean, at this level, when you open up your crown and your third eye, you are actually starting to pierce the meniscus and let the information flow directly into you. To be honest, this level is a lot like the previous level inasmuch as it relies on subtle manipulation of the CNS to *get your attention.* However, at the same time, it is more than simple emotional communication, because it is at this point that you actually begin to peek through the meniscus and let the ideas flow, if not freely, at least independently of your physical existence.

Exciting (!) because at this point, you are actually, carefully, touching The Waters of Consciousness. At this point, ideas (the stuff of The Fabric) are actually getting through. Not too much though. At this point, we're usually lacking in spiritual confidence so we still tread The Waters safely and with reserve. We may feel comfortable with subtle emotional communications, and we may even be okay with the occasional imposition of an idea, but we're still not too sure of ourselves and so we still maintain an ego barrier and an erroneous belief that it's "hard" to get a message through when in fact, when directly connected, it is very easy. Still, at this point, the illusion of separation is probably best, because the next step, which involves a totally *open channel,* can be quite the paranoid, freaky, soul cracking, discombobulating shocker for any of those still stuck with any of the nasty misconceptions I listed earlier in chapter two of this book.

Now, using your intuition and "sensing the ideas" in your head is definitely a step forward from listening to your body because it does allow the actual penetration of a spiritual thought once in a while. However, as you might guess, it is still limited. It is useful for a while so you can build up confidence in your ability to control the thought and image flow, but in the long run, if you stick with intuition, you are settling for the maintenance of an illusion and a restriction of communication. If you want to experience totally open communication with Spirit, you are going to have to move on from this at some point.

Don't forget. As with synchronicity and feeling, your purpose isn't to develop your intuition or get stuck in limited "psychic" mode. Your purpose is to develop confidence to the point where you can blow your connection wide open and reconnect with the **full** reality of Spirit.

That's the point.

Unfortunately, in this book I'm not going to take you to the point of wide-open connection. You know how to do it if you want to, but I wouldn't advise it at this point. There is a lot we need to consider and I don't have the space for it in this book so I'm leaving a discussion of full channeling out until I write *The Book of Magic*. This doesn't mean you shouldn't do it. If you want to, feel free.[36] However, for reasons that will become clear in *The Book of Magic*, I would advise that you not engage in channeling activity *for others* until you are certain you have a clear understanding of the mechanics and pitfalls.

One final set of comments. If you are a male reader I would like, at this point, to refer your consciousness to the chapter entitled **HERESY** later on in this book.

Why?

---

[36] If you do open to channel and you do find you need guidance, I will be posting advanced materials from *The Book of Magic* in the subscriber section of my website at www.michaelsharp.org

Well, because if you want to get past mere *synchronicity* as a form of spiritual communication, you are going to have to change your understanding of gender.

Why is that?

Well, it's a bit technical but basically it has to do with the "balance of energy" in your body. It is like this: Listening to your emotions, plugging into intuition, and gently expanding your mind into the glorious Fabric of Consciousness is a very soft, feminine, right brain sort of thing to do.

It is not very "objective."

It is not very "manly."

Therefore, the ability to communicate with Spirit is not often found in overly objective but energetically unbalanced, "manly" men.

Pourquoi?

Well, because intuition is the first *authentic* form of direct spiritual communication.

Because intuition is the first real penetration of the meniscus.

Because intuition is the first true connection to your higher self and, as such, intuition requires a functioning right brain hemisphere.

Why?

Because the only way to authentically communicate with spirit is from left hemisphere through right hemisphere and up.

And what does this have to do with gender?

Well, as explained in the chapter on HERESY, the right hemisphere functions best only when there's lots of yin energy around, and since yin has been erroneously associated with female, you need to stop suppressing the female side of you and open, if you haven't already, to the soft, feminine side of you.

It's not hard. Even if you're the manliest he-man of the universe, you can still learn to get in touch with your feminine side if you commit THE HERESY and admit you have a nurturing, loving, artistic, open, intuitive, emotional, soft feminine side. And you know what Mr. Man, I don't care how nervous or fidgety you might be here. Male or female, you can't get very far on your spiritual path of awakening unless you balance the energies.

Thankfully, it is easy to do. To do it, to balance your energies, do what you do with all things physical that you want to control. Simply intend and visualize. Say to yourself "I want to work with  balanced energies" and then find a visualization of the balance. The simplest (and therefore the most powerful) way that I've found is to use the ancient Chinese Yin/Yang symbol. The Yin/Yang is a perfect representation of the balance of energy and frankly, I can't think of a better way to visualize the balance of Yin/Yang than to use this symbol.

So use it. Picture the Yin/Yang symbol floating on its side above your head. Then visualize the symbol "passing through" your body as it energizes you with **balanced energies**. Trust your intuition here. See it rotating, see it cleansing, see it forcing muck out. See whatever you want, just keep balance in mind and open yourself to the transformation.

And don't be afraid.

Your behavioral repertoire will expand, and in a good way, but you're not going to be suddenly and mysteriously be drawn to your local gay bars. That's just paranoid, fear-based silliness. We choose our dominant gender expression, or cross expression, because that is where we are comfortable. That is what we enjoy. Leading a more balanced existence doesn't mean we stop being who we are. It just means we have more options and more powers available to us. That's all. So chill, open, and relax. It will do you a world of emotional and spiritual good. I promise.

HERESY

To the uneducated, an "A" is just three sticks.

~Winnie-the-Pooh

If you want my opinion, no great awakening, no penetration of the meniscus, no unfolding into glorious high consciousness would be complete without a heresy. Personally, I believe a heresy is necessary for awakening not so much for the sake of the heresy itself but because approaching the heresy is a kind of "test" of where you are at. Don't get me wrong. This is not a test in the sense that someone else is testing you to detect your worthiness or ability. Not at all! Heresy is a test of your progress forward viewable by you and useful only to you.

What do I mean by this?

Well, before you can understand what I'm talking about here, you need to understand about sacred truth. A sacred truth is basically an idea or concept so sacrosanct, authoritative, untouchable, and self-evident that to even question the truth causes people to either dismiss your sanity outright or consider bodily harm against you.

Heavy stuff.

A heresy occurs when someone, anyone, openly scoffs at, dismisses, or otherwise pisses on somebody's sacred truth.

A heresy is a big deal, especially in the eyes of the *faithful* who often see a heresy as an abomination, a horror, or a sin in the eyes of God (or Darwin). A heresy can be a scary event for everyone involved, but it is usually most uncomfortable for the person committing the heresy. When someone commits a heresy, their whole life is made extremely difficult, sometimes even impossible, by those who feel the need to "defend" the truth.

These days, people generally don't commit heresy. They used to more often, but the witch burnings and inquisitions put the "fear of authority" (a.k.a. The Fear of God) deep inside all of us and so now most of us stay well on the side of "compliant" and "believing" when it comes to the sacred truths in our life.

So that's heresy and sacred truth. The question now is, what exactly does heresy have to do with spiritual awakening? Let me put it this way. The ability to commit a heresy is a good test of where you are at on your own path back to divinity. A fully conscious, fully awakened individual will know that there is no such thing as a sacred truth, that Spirit makes **all** the rules and that, as a result, all the rules can be broken, bent, changed, or discarded at any time whatsoever. Where rules do exist, they exist as a result of consensus, because the *locals* (in the cosmic sense) agree the rule makes sense in the context of whatever it is they are trying to do. Therefore, you can judge how open and ready you are by your willingness to commit a heretical thought or act. If you can do that without fear, you're pretty much good to go. However, if you are presented with a heresy and you get all fidgety, defensive, offensive, or even violent, you know you've got work to do.

So, what's a good heresy to test yourself against? Well, it really depends on your social-cultural context. It depends on your religious background, the way your parents raised you, whether you have a post-secondary education, and things like that. If you are scientist, there are a few sacred truths you could bounce yourself against (e.g., the myth of objectivity, the necessity of peer review, the superiority of the rational mind, things like that). It really all depends, and it is hard to specify or give examples. A few hundred years ago it would have been easier. A few hundred years ago there was a lot more homogeneity in belief systems, so we all tended to agree that certain things were heretical. Nowadays it seems there's no such agreement. What's heresy to a scientist may not be heresy to a dogmatic Christian and vice versa. If you're not sure about your own state of openness, ask your Spirit guides to present you with a heresy and then pay attention. I'm sure something will come up.

Now, if you don't want to go to the trouble of digging information from your guides, I do have one global heresy that yet remains. There is one idea that pretty much everybody on this planet can agree is sacrosanct and untouchable, self evident, divinely inspired and even given as law by God. That idea is *gender.*

Let's think about it for a few moments, shall we?

Everybody on this planet believes in the importance, nay sacredness, of gender. Scientists, priests, popes, magi, pundits, politicians, and even the average Joe down in the pub find common ground here. Everybody believes that gender is the crux of our existential being-ness.

You cannot argue this point.

I mean, gender differentiation, gender duality, is so important that our belief in the power of gender is not left to chance. Indoctrination begins at birth. Boys get blue, girls get pink[37] and it just gets worse from there. This blatant, unabashed, bold-faced attempt to separate the genders continues on through infanthood, childhood, adolescence, and even adulthood where everything from the cloths you wear to the games you play and the foods you eat are gender loaded with all sorts of "boys do this" and "girls do that" nonsense.

For some reason,[38] we are taught from day one that gender is some kind of big fat sacred deal. And we buy it! By adolescence, gender has become a defining category. By adolescence, we see everything in terms of gender. By the time we are adults, gender has been *burned* into the neural pathways of our brains.

If you think about it, it's weird.

Why is it a sin for a boy to wear pink?

———————————————

[37] *As if* it makes some kind of big difference.
[38] The reason is explained in my *Book of Life: Ascension and the Divine World Order.*

Why do only girls get to wear pretty things?

What's the BFFD anyway?

And over some minor bodily differences, too!

A testicle, an ovary, some boobs, and a slightly different shape.

What is the big deal?

Well, I'll tell ya.

There ain't no big deal.

In fact, allow me to be the first person to say that in the cosmic scheme of things, in an unfolding of creation sort of way, in an eternal Fabric of Consciousness, "logos of the creator," thing-a-ma-bob, thing-a-ma-jingy sort of way, gender just isn't that important. The truth is, there are no deep mystical meanings, no esoteric secrets, no profound evolutionary significance, and no determining biological influences behind the sex of your physical vehicle. In the cosmic scheme of things, gender amounts to no more than your preferred means of experiencing the pleasures of sex (and also your willingness to experience the joys and difficulties of childbirth).

That's all.

It's a question of boink partners and nothing more.

And frankly, I don't care what the scientists or the priests or the psychiatrists or the hob knobs or the bob wobbles have to say about it.

I know.

In terms of spirit/consciousness/god, gender is nothing.

Despite what those loopy priests tell you, God isn't male.

Consciousness has no sex.

Bottom line, in the cosmic everything of our collective divinity, there's simply no room for gender.

Now, I know what you're thinking.

"Michael, you're obviously crazy."

"Michael, can't you see?"

"Male/female."

"Positive/negative."

"Yin/Yang."

"From electricity to electrons, it's everywhere!"

"Isn't it?"

Well, I admit it.

It does appear to be everywhere, at least in *this* physical universe, and at least during the time period we are capable, with our limited physical instruments, of accurately observing.

It's true.

Yin/Yang, positive/negative are important, in this physical universe. But despite that fact, get this. Talking about positive and negatives charges on an atomic particle, or talking about the yin and yang energies of this physical universe, is not the same as talking about gender. One has to do with, well, energy and the other has to do with whether or not you are capable of incubating a baby. They are totally different things and to think otherwise, to equate them as if there is an equal sign in the middle, is a *non sequitur* of biblical proportions.

They are not the same.

Yin does not equate to the female body.

Yang does not equate to the male body.

Which isn't to say that Yin and Yang aren't important for the body.

They are important.

Yin and Yang are energies. They are two sides of the same coin, *two complementary aspects* of *prana, chi, the Breath of God, The Waters of Creation,* or whatever you want to call it. A body, any body, from solar rock to human being, uses Yin and Yang to maintain itself and create its world. Male or female, young or old, animal, vegetable or mineral, in this universe you must draw on both energies to function well. If you only draw one side of the energetic coin, you are not running at full potential. You need both.

If it helps, think of your Immortal Soul as an electrician responsible for keeping "things" (creation, the world, your body, the building downtown), empowered. In order to do the job of electrician, in order to bring light into the darkness, or bring power to a factory, the electrician must harness and control the energy (a.k.a. electricity, in the lingo of the trade). Harnessing and controlling the electricity is accomplished, as we all learn in grade school, by manipulation of the "positive" and "negative" poles of the electrical force.

Think about it for a moment.

If you don't have both positive and negative, if you don't have both yin and yang, there's no electrical flow. Without positive and negative, there's no energetic movement. In creative terms, you're powered down, ineffective, and impotent.[39] The bottom line, in order to bring power to a house or a factory or even a physical body, the "electrician," the soul, the animating consciousness, must plug both negative and positive prongs into the appropriate receptacles. In other words, you need both yin and yang energies.

I talk about fully empowering your body in more detail in *The Dossier of the Ascension.* For now it is enough for me to emphasize, and for you to remember, that gender has nothing to do with anything more than sex and procreation.

---

[39] I suppose this might be one explanation for why gender indoctrination isn't left to chance. Who wants powerful slaves?

Got it?

So, if you want to advance into full spiritual power, begin the process of opening to the opposite energies immediately. You can use the visualization I suggested in the chapter on *Roadside Communication* or come up with a version suitable for yourself. The important thing is the intent behind the visualization. The intent should be to balance the energies and open to the opposite forces. If you are male, this means cultivating the yin energies. If you are female, this means cultivating your yang energies. The visualization only helps you maintain consistent intent, so come up with a visualization that is clear to you. That's all you have to do.

Just forget about gender and remember, yin and yang energies are merely **complementary** sides of the same creative force. Your body, your mind (your brain) requires both. Begin the process of bringing them together by embracing that which you have rejected, and, word of advice, don't be too much in a rush.

I advise that you go slow.

You have been excluding what you consider to be the "opposite" energy for centuries. As a result, coming into contact with the powerful and "frightening" opposite can require care and attention, so take your time and don't do anything that you aren't comfortable doing. If you do experience fear, discomfort, or weird ideas,[40] remember my advice on trust. On the other side of this heresy is a light, love and power that has been denied to you for centuries. If you want that back (and who wouldn't?), trust in the process and get over your gender based fears. Remember, sex and gender are one thing. Yin and yang, positive and negative, are something else.

And besides, what male in this world wouldn't benefit from the nurturing, receptive, and open orientations that yin energies provide? What female wouldn't benefit from the active, powerful, confident, "get it done" driving energies of yang?

We need both, we need both, we need both.

It is time we live a balanced life in the true sense of that word.

Trust me on this.

Your health, your piece of mind, your power, even your ability to create in this world will benefit greatly by a rebalancing of energy.

Remember, your soul is the electrician, your body is a temple.

Plug it in, plug it in, plug it in.

---

[40] For example, you think I'm trying to make you gay or something.

DIET AND NUTRITION

When having a smackerel of
something with a friend, don't eat
so much that you get stuck in the
doorway trying to get out.
~Winnie-the-Pooh

In closing this book, I want to say a few things about diet. If you haven't heard it before, you need to hear it now. What you put in your body, how you *fuel* your soul's physical vehicle, is important. The bottom line is, if you are going to be serious about this "spiritual awakening" thing, if you want to make best progress on this path of empowerment, if you want to stay healthy and attain full bodily power, you are going to have to pay close attention to what you put into your body. As I emphasized earlier, awakening your body and mind, powering up and driving safely on the roadways of creation is not about soul evolution or moral evolution or being a better child of God or declaring Jesus Christ as your savior or anything like that. Spiritual awakening is about bringing your full consciousness into your physical body and learning to use the physical vehicle properly. Basically, spiritual awakening is about turning on your engines, firing up your chakra systems,[41] and fine-

---

[41] I explain charkas in more detail in my *Book of Life* and *Dossier of The Ascension*.

tuning your physical body and mind enough to allow your soul, your higher self, your full consciousness, a.k.a. the "divinity within," full expression.

Tune in, turn on, power up as I like to say.

Bottom line, spiritual awakening is a <u>physical</u> process and as such, you have to treat it like any other physical process. If you want the physical process to work, you have to take care of it and fuel it properly. So, if you want my advice, treat your body/mind with respect.

Treat your soul's vehicle (your body) like the *temple* that it is.

Breathe properly, balance the energies, drive safely, and don't put toxic junk into the gas tank. You wouldn't put garbage in your car's gas tank would you? So why do think it is appropriate to put junk in your body's gas tank?

Think about this.

How the heck is your body and mind going to handle the high vibration of your spirit if it's not fed and watered properly?

Answer?

It's not.

Bottom line, your body and mind need to be strong and while it is true that your body is a finely tuned, self-balancing instrument of creation, it can only deal with so much. If you are going to feed it constant garbage, if you are going to blithely ignore its nutritional requirements, and if you are going to harass it with excessive drugs, alcohol, and sugar, it is going to break down eventually and when it does, it won't be pretty.

Remember this.

What you put in your mouth goes to your brain, your Central Nervous System, and to the rest of your body. If you want your body and mind to work properly, put good fuel in, **especially these days**. Proper diet is important at all times, but the closer we get to 2012, the more people awaken, and the more of your own high consciousness enters into your body and mind, the more important proper diet is going to be. As your higher consciousness embraces the cells of your body, and as the energy levels of this planet continue to rise and finally skyrocket, your body and mind will do a lot better if you feed and water them properly. When you do, when you take care of them and keep them operating at peak efficiency, energy will flow, toxins will be released, cells will regenerate, and the entire fabric of your physical and mental existence will just work better.

So, question before us now is, how do you keep your body and mind healthy?

Well, I say, listen to the experts. They say, eat a proper diet and exercise.

So do that.

Exercise and eat properly.

Now, exercise is self explanatory; but, what's a proper diet? It's an important question and it can be hard to figure out a "right answer" these days. The "experts" are still battling about what's best and the diet gurus are all keeping their "diet secrets" a secret so they can sell them for profit. However, based on my own experience, and a little bit of common sense nutrition, I think it's safe to say that a healthy dietary regime consists, in addition to regular exercise, rest, lots of water, and a balanced diet. Allow me to elaborate on each of these three points for a few moments.

As you already know, rest is important so the body can regenerate. We all need lots of sleep, adults, yes, but children and teenagers even more so. Children need a lot of sleep because their bodies and brains are growing and teenagers need a lot of sleep because their brains and bodies are growing. Children and teenagers suck in loads of energy during the day (through food, through breathing) and use that energy at night to transform and grow. You must give their growing bodies and minds the rest they need. Children need between ten and twelve hours of rest each day, teenagers twelve or more.[42] The sleep they get is

---

[42] I realize that these sleep figures interfere with the "productive sphere" of this planet (i.e., the workday). Tough luck. The truth is, the productive sphere of this planet, i.e., the workweek, is hostile to your physical, mental, and spiritual health. This will change as the planet ascends and the world comes to be more in tune with the truth of all things. Until then, do you what you can to get the rest that your body needs.

critical. If your children aren't getting enough sleep, you are stunting their physical and mental grown. Indeed, for the child's body and the teenager's mind, sleep is more important than socialization, soccer, swimming, music lessons, or whatever else you do for your kids. Children need to go to bed early (especially if they wake up early) and teenagers should be allowed full cycles, within parental reason.

Sleep is important for adults as well, not so much because we need the sleep to grow and develop but because it is during our sleep cycles that our bodies recover from the physical, social, political, psychological, and spiritual assaults we endure every day we exist within The System. Sleep is where a lot of the toxic negativity we experience during the day is washed away and where your cells regenerate themselves. As a general principle, I would say that the uglier your day has been, the more sleep you'll need at night in order to recover. Personally, I would consider seven or eight hours as a minimum. I would recommend more if you're doing any "heavy lifting," if you find yourself working in toxic environments, or if you feel you need the extra rest. A very few of us may need less, but in general, we all benefit from nice long sleeps. Sleep is critical. If you are not getting enough sleep, you are not allowing your body to recover, and if you don't allow your body to recover, then over the short (and longer term) your body will weaken, sicken, and die.

Now, the other thing you need to do for your general health, and especially as you go through the awakening and ascension process, is drink more water. In fact, drink lots of water. Consciousness, vibration, your soul, your light, your higher self, whatever you want to call it, is bright and powerful, while the cells of your body (and your body includes your brain) are fragile and easily damaged by the intensity of your consciousness. Think about X-rays for a moment. Compared to your consciousness, X-rays aren't a particular potent form of energy. Even so, an X-ray can cause your body's cells to *pop* and fizzle. Imagine the strain that occurs as your consciousness settles in and "fills up" your body! In order to avoid the strain on your cells, drink more water.

How much water?

Well, everybody's needs are different, of course. Your water intake will vary by body size, temperature, altitude, exercise levels, current health, the amount of sleep you're getting, the type of food you're eating (more toxic foods require more water to flush), and any previous cellular damage done. The Institute of Medicine advises roughly about thirteen cups of liquid a day for men and nine cups a day for women.[43] Consider this your minimum daily intake. Remember, your body is 70% water. Don't ignore this advice.

Finally, in addition to better sleep and more fluid intake, you need to eat better. Ideally this means a diet rich in low

---

[43] http://www.mayoclinic.com/health/water/NU00283

fat protein, fruit, vegetables, nuts, and smoothies[44] with **no** processed foods whatsoever (or in extremely limited quantities) and no "white bread" or pastas. Your body needs a certain amount of protein, and since our current commercial delivery system is set up to deliver protein via dead animal flesh, you're going to need to eat some meat. Consult a dietician about how much. However, keep in mind this fact. If you are North American, chances are you are currently eating way too much meat, so be prepared to cut down. Going Vegan is a good option if you get the protein you need. It is hard now, but it will get easier with time. You may also want to consider drastically reducing your intake of dairy. Some people are starting to think that the pasteurization process is dangerous and even if it is not, dairy animals are routinely injected with hormones and other chemicals and you want to keep that stuff out of your ascending body.

I also recommend you give up coffee and other forms of CNS stimulation immediately. Decaf is fine (Swiss Water process preferred), and a regular coffee once in a while is okay, but consuming caffeine at the rates many of us drink it these days is not. Coffee is bad for you for lots of health and spiritual reasons. It is a drug, for one, and like any drug it's unhealthy and dangerous to consume in large

---

[44] Smoothies are better than juices for a couple of reasons. More nutrition is retained in the pulp and the pulp prevents the sugars from being absorbed too quickly into your bloodstream causing glucose spikes.

quantities on a regular basis. It also mucks around with your metabolism and speeds up your analytical brain processes. Now, speeding up your linear processes can be a good thing if you're working in a left-brain, linear type job. However, it is a bad thing in terms of opening yourself intuitively and spiritually. Bottom line is, if you want to open that channel of yours wider than mere intuition, you need to consider cutting out the stimulants and *slowing down* that chatty left-brain of yours. Although we don't talk about full-blown channeling in this book, you'll get to that point sooner or later. Might as well start the process of riding your body of addictions now.[45]

Now, I know that some of you may be going into shock at this point given how radical a diet change I may be suggesting, but what can I say?

Tough.

I don't know what it's like in other parts of the world, but our average North American diet and lifestyle is about as toxic as you can get. In North America, we are literally poisoning ourselves with nutritionally void and heavily damaged processed foods. We don't sleep well, we don't drink enough water, we eat crap, and we fill up daily with

---

[45] On a related note, electronics have the same "dampening" effect on your spiritual connections to consciousness. Reducing your exposure to the fields caused by electronic devices is always a good thing. Turn off computers and other devices when not in use.

chemical stimulants designed to keep us going despite the fact that our bodies are on the verge of breaking down and we should be stopping and resting in order to repair. Is it any wonder that as we age we bloat up, dry up, crack up, and break down? It doesn't have to be that way. It shouldn't be that way. As many are already beginning to find out, our bodies can stay healthy and functioning well beyond the arbitrary checkpoints of the "labor force script" we follow as we travel through the lifecycle. The truth is, your body and mind can stay healthy as long as you want, as long as you feed, water, and rest.

As far as the transition to a healthy diet goes, this doesn't have to be a dramatic transition. You can go slow. You can do a little bit at a time. Move from regular coffee to decaf or green tea. Add a piece of fruit in the morning and at lunch. Replace the meat on your sandwiches with tomatoes, guacamole, and sprouts every once in a while. Drink more plain water without the additives (pop, caffeine beverages, juices) and when you do drink other than water, drink smoothies, herbal teas, and the like.

Little steps is fine.

You do not have to sacrifice.

Just set your intent to transition to a healthier lifestyle and diet and then **make the right choices when they come your way**. Keep your intent pure and persistent. Visualize a healthy body and mind and the transition to a healthier eating style will occur naturally, spontaneously, and with minimal effort.[46] Even better, it will get easier over time. Even now, grocers, restaurants, and other food-type establishments are starting to provide healthier alternatives. These alternatives will only grow and become more visible as more of us make the choice to live healthy lifestyles.

You'll see.

A new marketplace will emerge as if by magic.

---

[46] As an example, consider this. Just recently my entire family (two adults, three kids) suddenly, with no effort, and no sense of sacrifice, gave up drinking cow's milk. It happened spontaneously one day. We all simply decided, after discussing hormones and other additives in the milk, that we weren't going to drink cow's milk anymore and so we simply stopped buying it. We substituted soymilk for a while but even our consumption of that has dropped dramatically. Of course, we are not totally abstinent. We still drink the Moo Juice on occasion, and still have ice cream treats, but as far as daily consumption, no more—and nobody misses it. Interestingly, all we did to achieve this effortless transformation was intend a better diet. As we did that, opportunities (created via our intention) for better eating came floating by us. As they did, we simply seized the opportunities as presented. The result? Effortless dietary transformation! You just can't ask for better than that.

A final comment: this chapter is too short to give comprehensive nutritional advice and can really only function as an introduction. This is not a problem though because these days, more and more dieticians and food experts are recognizing the dangers of processing, sugars, fats, huge meals (as opposed to grazing behavior),[47] and the like. Read and educate yourself about healthy eating patterns. If you are eating properly, your body should settle into a normal weight with only moderate activity. If you are not eating properly, your body will gain weight, or lose too much weight, and you will be sickly and prone to disease and depression. Judge eating patterns for yourself by observing your body's physical and mental responses to the food you eat. Figure out what foods work for you and stick with them. As an example, I consume only in limited quantities anything that makes me feel *heavy.* You do the same. Stay away from things that make you feel icky.

Pay attention to your body. Find your own way. This really is the only way forward.

---

[47] It is ironic, is it not, that although we've been taught that we are a carnivorous species, hunters and gatherers always fighting against scarcity, nevertheless our bodies function best when we "graze" (i.e., eat in small quantities throughout the day)? It's as if we are descended not from a world of violence and scarcity but from a world of plenty where food was always to hand and the body never went without sustenance for any significant length of time. How else do we explain this persistent physical adaptation to grazing behavior?

A TIP OF THE HAT

Sometimes, if you stand on the bottom rail of a bridge and lean over to watch the river slipping slowly away beneath you, you will suddenly know everything there is to be known.

~ Winnie the Pooh

And so we come to the end of this introductory spiritual text. At this point, I would like to take the opportunity to thank you all for following along this far. I appreciate your effort and the time you have given in order to read this book through to the end, so thanks! It is my wish that the time you have spent here has been both awakening and empowering. In fact, it was my intent when writing this book that it would awaken and empower, so if you feel more awake, more stimulated, more knowledgeable, and more empowered now that you have finished this book, wonderful! I am pleased and honored to have a played a part in your journey back to divinity.

If you have enjoyed this book, if you have found it to be uplifting and awakening, and if you want to read more of my work, then I am very happy to say there is more. I have written six adult and children's books prior to this one and plan to write at least three more. As with this book, all the books I write go into important details about your spiritual awakening and empowerment process, details designed to help you rapidly remember the core truth of your divinity. Personally, I don't think you'll get a better introduction to your own divinity than through the books that I write. However, I'll be honest with you up front. As much as I want you to buy my books, you don't have to. Like I said earlier, as long as you keep the tools in this book handy, you won't have any trouble. You'll be able to tread water and "rise with the tide," so to speak. However, I realize that some of you may be impatient, some of you may want to *go ahead* in order to help out and lead the way for others, and some may want to go beyond basic knowledge and proceed with more advanced study. If you're one of those people, then by all means read my other books. All my books are grounded, easy to read, packed with useful information, and written with the single-minded intent that they be the most powerful, most effective, and most successful books on spiritual awakening and empowerment ever written.

No compromise.

No strings attached.

I promise.

In closing, I would like to offer you one final "gift." In the appendix of this book you will find my *Parable of the Garden.* As you may already be aware, our current belief systems, our current faiths, our current spiritualities, are riddled with justifications for hierarchy, inequality, poverty, injustice, and woe. Science, religion, or spirituality, it doesn't matter. Whatever your particular dogma, you are told you suffer ("we" suffer, "they" suffer) because you deserve it. You suffer because you are unworthy, because you ate a bad apple, because it's your "karma," or because you are weak and the strong deserve the reward. Whatever the excuse is, it doesn't matter. When you boil it right down to its essence, you are taught to accept the ugly state of the world because there is some divine, natural, genetic, or spiritual reason for it.

Frankly, that's all nonsense.

The world is in the story state it's in not because of some divine plan or cosmic karmic machine, but because of the choices that people like you, I, and (most importantly) the people with horde the power make. The bottom line is, it is you and I, the ones who follow and go along, the ones who rule and set the course, who make the choices that create this world. It's we who do it, not God or nature. In the divine world of Spirit, there's no reason for suffering. There's no reason for poverty. There's no justification for war and it should all end right now with no "ifs," "ands" or "buts" about it.

No more freaking excuses.

It must end right now.

So where do we start?

Well, in my opinion we need to start with new stories that don't justify suffering or qualify the terrible condition of this world. We need new stories that don't let us off the hook by speaking about sin or karma, hierarchy or entitlement. We need new stories that speak to us, in no uncertain terms, about our **unity**, our **divine purpose**, and our magnificent **power** in Spirit. We need a new story that empowers each and every one of us to make a difference and change this world. As it so happens, I have a story (or two) just like that and I'm including it in the appendix to this book. What follows at the end of this chapter is my *Parable of The Garden.* As you will see when you read it, this is an entirely new story that does not justify. Within *The Parable of The Garden* you will find an entirely new theological foundation for existing in this world that contains no justification for inequality, poverty, hierarchy, war, hatred, violence, or evil of any form. Here you will find no deep philosophical support of "darkness," no biblical justification of divine madness, and no way out of the fundamental truth of your (our) primary responsibility for creation. This is a new story, a true story, and a transformative story that puts the power of change and the power of God directly into your hands.

So, open your heart, open your mind, and read The Parable of The Garden for what it is—a new story of your origin and purpose that takes you a step forward on the path back to the divinity within you.

It is my gift to you.

Consider it only the first of many welcome home presents from me, your guide back to divinity, Michael Sharp.

THE PARABLE OF THE GARDEN[48]

Allow me to speak to you a few moments now. Allow me to tell you a story, a parable, about *The Garden*.

Imagine a garden unlike any garden you have ever seen on this earth.

Imagine a garden full of flowers and trees, of brilliant sights and sounds, of sparkling diamond water, and clear emerald forests.

Imagine a garden of unbelievable fertility, variety, and bounty.

Imagine a garden where life flourishes in peace, love, and joy.

Imagine a garden where the only emotions are contentment, bliss, happiness, and love.

Imagine a garden where only beauty exists.

Call this garden The Garden of Eden, Shambhala,[49] or even Heaven if you like, for indeed it was all these and more.

---

[48] For a video presentation of this parable, see www.michaelsharp.org/parableofthegarden
[49] Shambhala is the Tibetan version of *Heaven On Earth*.

Imagine, and when you can imagine all these things at once, put them together and multiply them a million times and you will have *The Garden.*

A place of unimaginable splendor and glory.

…

Now let me be crystal clear here.

In *The Garden* there is no pain and no suffering.

In The Garden, there is no sadness.

There is no war.

There is no hatred.

There is no "sin."

The Garden is perfect in every way and will always remain so, for this is the way The Lightwalkers, the beings of pure love and light who inhabit The Garden, want it.

Ah, The Lightwalkers.

Shining, glorious suns of creation.

Brilliant and blinding to behold.

When they created *The Garden,* they created it as a reflection of their perfect, Light-filled, love filled nature.

Each heart's desire fulfilled.

Perfection in every way and a mighty great place to live, let me tell you.

But, you know, things get boring and so one day a few of the Lightwalkers (let us call them *The Explorers*) thought to themselves that maybe, just maybe, a change was needed.

"Maybe things could **be** better?" they said.

"Maybe we could have more beautiful flowers and trees, more brilliant sights and sounds."

"Maybe we could have more love and more light and more glory."

"Maybe!"

So, they put a plan together and submitted it to The Elders, and they said with great excitement...

"Look at our plan."

"Isn't it cool?"

"Isn't it wonderful?"

"Isn't it amazing?"

And of course, The Elders had to agree, for The Plan was beautiful and amazing and glorious and if it worked...

"If the thing could be done..." they thought.

"It would be something completely different."

"It would mean more of everything that The Lightwalkers love so much."

"Of course, The Plan would require a lot of work and effort," The Elders thought.

"The Plan would require mucking around in the darkness outside The Garden and that is cause for pause," said The Elders.

"It would be no picnic," The Elders said.

"There would be no partying."

"It would not be a holiday in paradise."

"You are, after all, descending into darkness" The Elders said.

"It's not going to be fun."

"*There is nothing in darkness,*" the Elders warned.

"There is no love."

"There is no light."

"There is no power."

Ah, but the pups who brought The Plan didn't seem to mind so much the sacrifice and so the Elders said, "Why not?"

And besides, if *The Explorers* could pull it off, what a "**wow**" that would be…

And so the explorers packed their bags, bid their tearful goodbyes, walked the long walk out past The Garden Gate and into the darkness, and **disappeared** from view.

* poof *

Which worried The Lightwalkers who stayed back more than a little bit.

It was kinda dramatic, after all.

It was kinda abrupt.

It was like being suddenly cut off from a part of yourself.

And it was without precedent.

It was disturbing.

But they trusted, and tried not to worry.

They waited and they watched.

They watched and waited, and when they had waited and watched to the limit of their patience, they started to talk about sending out a search party.

What else was there to do?

Something had to be done.

What if something had, inconceivably, gone wrong?

But, just as they were about to form the search party "It" happened.

All of a sudden, the silence and the blackness of the darkness were broken by a flash and a sound.

Then, there was another flash and another sound.

Then another.

And another, and pretty soon the flashes were like lightning and the sound was like thunder.

And the Lightwalkers breathed a sigh of relief.

The Work had begun.

And thus did the work go on.

While the Lightwalkers continued to exist in Joy and Bliss, the Explorers worked hard in the darkness. There were flashes and there was thunder, there were crashes and there was rumble and every once in a while a crackle of fire danced across the skin of the darkness.

It was an exciting light-and-sound show like never before seen.

The raw energy of it was contagious, and soon many of those who had stayed behind just couldn't stand by watching anymore.

They packed their bags and ran off into the dark to help.

And that fed the fire. And the lighting flashed brighter, and the thunder crashed louder, and a fire crackled over the skin of the dark until...

All of a sudden...

Nothing.

Suddenly...

All the flashing and all the thunder just stopped, just like that.

One moment, chaos and the next, nothing.

At that point, the Lightwalkers who had stayed behind looked at each other.

They were puzzled.

They waited, but the silence continued.

"What could have happened?" they asked themselves.

"Has something gone wrong?" they wondered.

They waited, and they waited, and they waited to the limits of their worry and when they surpassed their limit, they formed a search party.

After all, this was highly irregular, unusual, and worrisome.

This was without precedent.

Something could be wrong.

But then, just as the search party was getting ready to leave The Garden, with a flash of lightning and a sound of thunder, the chaos began anew.

Just like before, lightning, thunder and fire crackled over the dark.

The work had begun once again.

And thus did the work go on.

There were flashes and thunder and fire, and the Lightwalkers gazed in fascination and amazement.

It was a show unlike any other.

And much more exciting than before.

More energy.

More power.

More vibration.

It was a pulsating energy ball...

Like an oscillating star going Nova...

And it was very exciting.

In fact, it was so exciting that wave after wave of Lightwalkers, overcome by a childlike exuberance, jumped into the darkness without even bothering to pack. As they did that, they fed the fire. And lightning flashed and thunder rolled and fire crackled and then, all of a sudden...

FLASH

...and then...

...DARKNESS...

...and then...

...SILENCE...

...and then...

NOTHING...

The Lightwalkers were startled by this.

They looked at each other; they were puzzled.

They waited and wondered and worried, only this time...

This time it was obvious.

Something had gone wrong.

So, they called for volunteers and sent a search party out into the darkness, and just as the Searchers disappeared from view, the Explorers came screaming out of the darkness.

"Did you see that?" they said breathless.

"Wasn't it awesome?" they exclaimed with excitement.

"Did you see that?" they said over and over again, shaking all over.

"DID YOU SEE THAT?"

"We almost did it," they laughed.

"We almost had it."

"But we need your help," they said, shaking their shoulders.

"There was too much," they gasped.

"There were too many," they exclaimed.

"And it was too soon!"

"WE NEED YOUR HELP!"

And, of course, the Lightwalkers who remained in The Garden agreed.

What else could they do?

The Explorers were obviously onto something big and exciting.

So they said, "How can we help?"

And at that, the Explorers paused and thought about it for a few moments and then said, "Well, let's see."

"As you can see," said the Explorers, "it is extremely black down there and we have a hard time seeing."

"Sometimes we get lost in the darkness."

"Sometimes we get confused."

"So it would be great," said the Explorers, if some of you could act as **guides** for us."

"You know, point us in the right direction if we seem to be stumbling around too much."

Now, at hearing that, hands shot up everywhere.

Volunteers, let us call them *The Guides*, jumped at the chance.

After all, who wouldn't?

Who wouldn't want a special role in this divinely inspired plan?

"We will help," said The Guides.

"We will provide assistance as required and we will walk with you in the shadows and the valleys."

Hearing this, the Explorers smiled and nodded.

Then they turned and paused and scratched their chins and after a few moments they said, "There is something else."

"As you know, there is so no light down there in the dark and it is really hard to see what we are doing."

"What is worse, when things start to get real crazy, we start to forget what we're doing and get all turned around in the chaos."

"So it would be great," said the Explorers, "if some of you could hold a light for us.

And of course, hands shot up everywhere.

Volunteers, let us call them *The Lightholders*, jumped at the opportunity.

Seeing the enthusiasm, the Explorers smiled and thanked them.

Then, they turned and paused and scratched their chins and after a few moments they said, "There is one final thing."

"As we keep saying, it's awfully dark down there, and there are so many working on The Plan now, and the energy levels are at such fantastic levels, that it can easily get out of control."

"We have to prevent that from happening," said the Explorers, "until everything's ready.

"What we need," they said, "is someone to keep the lid on until it's time."

And of course, there was no shortage of volunteers despite the difficulty of this particular job.

And so, the Explorers, the Guides, the Lightholders, and the new Energy Keepers went out into the darkness to work.

Those who stayed behind watched and waited and for a long time they saw nothing move, but this time they didn't get worried.

They knew everything was under control and so they waited, without a limit to their patience, until a shout sprang up.

"THERE!" someone screamed.

"THERE in the darkness."

"Did you see that?"

"Did you see that?"

 "SPARKS!!!!!"

Everybody looked and, sure enough, they could see sparks in the darkness.

To no one's surprise, these sparks quickly grew and soon, lightning, thunder, and fire crackled.

The light and the energy were intense.

The power expanded and grew and then, just when it seemed like the energy and fire had reached their ultimate, the energy started to hum and pulse, expanding and contracting like some giant cosmic egg.

The energy would expand outward, reaching a raging crescendo of intense flame.

Then it would back off from the peak.

Then, another cycle with a higher peak.

And then another cycle, a higher peak.

And then another.

And then another.

It was like a giant pulsating balloon of energy being puffed up and then deflated, puffed up and deflated, each time the balloon straining against some unseen barrier that kept it contained within its own boundaries.

The Lightwalkers watched the undulation in fascination.

Wide-eyed.

Awe-filled.

Never growing tired of the spectacle.

But then...

After what seemed like an eternity (but was really only a few moments in the creative consideration of Spirit),

"It" happened.

Just as the crackling ball of fire was at its most intense ever, just as it seemed as if the heat from this "forge of creation" could not get any more intense, "It" happened.

The Lightwalkers saw it happen.

There...

In the heat of an already intense fire...

In the cracking of an engorged cellular balloon,

There....

A single brilliant explosion of light...

And then another.

And then another.

And then ten more,

And then a thousand more.

And then ten thousand.

And then a million.

And then six billion.

And then...

A crack on the surface....

Then tendrils of fire racing over the skin of the darkness.

Then an explosion.

Then eyes widening.

Light. Love. Wonder.

Beauty. Glory. Power.

Happiness. Joy. Bliss.

Glorious.

No words.

Weeping.

And then, just as it seemed the Lightwalkers would be overcome by the glory, The Procession began.

Amongst cheering and laughter and celebration and glory, those who had entered into the darkness began to emerge.

The Explorers...

The Energy Keepers...

The Lightholders...

The Guides....

Even The Search Party...

Even though they had gone in only a moment before it happened.

They all started to return, and they did so in chariots of magnificent, brilliant gold, like angels of fire in an undefeatable Army of God.

And with them, with us, comes *The Fire* and the transformation and, in fulfillment of The Plan, a new Garden more glorious than anything we have ever imagined before.

LIGHTNING PATH BOOKS BY MICHAEL SHARP

I just finished THE BOOK OF LIFE, DOSSIER OF THE ASCENSION, and THE SONG OF CREATION. What an extraordinary contribution you've made to the enlightenment of our little species! These are the best spiritual books I've read since Yogananda's commentary on the Gita.
William T. Hathaway author of Summer Snow, and award winning author.

What is *The Lightning Path? The Lightning Path* is Avatar Publication's and Michael Sharp's name for his "system" of spiritual enlightenment and empowerment. The system consists of articles, books, poems, and other "vectors" of spiritual communication designed to lift your consciousness out of the 3-D world of duality, illusion, and maya in which you are trapped, and into the beautiful and powerful world of your own high spiritual consciousness. It is all about your spiritual enlightenment and empowerment.

Some teachers might like to tell you that doing this, i.e., becoming enlightened and empowered, is extremely difficult, or that you have to work off lifetimes of karma in order to be worthy. That's not true. It doesn't need to take that long. In fact, spiritual enlightenment and empowerment are easy. At the most, and under the very worst of circumstances, full enlightenment and empowerment will take you about two years. Chances are good that for you, it will take even less time.

Curious? It is very easy. All you have to do is a bit of reading, a few seconds of meditation a day, and a little bit of clearing. A little bit of time out of your busy schedule, a little bit of space in your private life, and miracles will be performed! How fast you get through everything, how fast you complete your **great awakening,** depends entirely on you, but once you get going you will be drawn forward by the reality of your power and your own exuberance and excitement at the glorious return to self and power that you will find on *The Lightning Path.*

Michael's *Lightning Path* books are available directly from Avatar Publications, (http://www.avatarpublication.com), Amazon.com and its international derivatives, Barnes and Noble, your local retailer, and wherever fine books are sold. *Lightning Path* books are listed below for your convenience.

THE SONG OF CREATION: THE STORY OF GENESIS

The Song of Creation is the complete and canonical story of creation. From *the beginning* to the ascension of this universe, our collective path, and your role in it, *The Song of Creation* provides a powerful cadence to the work of Michael Sharp and is a testament to the power of Michael's pen. Empower yourself and return to The Garden. **ISBN: 978-09737401-6-5.**

THE BASIC BOOK: CONCEPTS AND TECHNIQUES FOR SUCCESSFUL SPIRITUAL PRACTICE

The Basic Book is a spiritual primer. This book provides all the groundwork and basic spiritual techniques you need in order to awaken from your long spiritual sleep with speed and efficiency. Learn about the importance of breathing, visualization, and trust. Learn how to open spiritual communication with your higher self and your guides. Learn about channeling, the importance of diet, balance, and more. *The Basic Book* is a masterful introduction to your glorious spiritual power. **ISBN: 978-1-897455-74-6.**

DOSSIER OF THE ASCENSION: A PRACTICAL GUIDE TO CHAKRA ACTIVATION AND KUNDALINI AWAKENING

The *Dossier of the Ascension* is the owner's manual for your physical body. With the skill that only a master can bring, Michael Sharp provides all the guidance you need in order to shrug off the chains that keep you away from your spiritual power and birthright. With *The Dossier* in hand, you will quickly and efficiently throw off the fears and misconceptions that keep your chakras blocked and your kundalini in bondage. Learn how to activate your chakras and stay activated. Learn what to expect as you move from inefficient co-creator to powerful co-creator of the physical universe around you. Learn how easy it is to overcome blockage and attain the holy grail of Spiritual attainment—*full chakra activation and safe kundalini activation. The Dossier* is a must read for anybody serious about spiritual empowerment or ascension. **ISBN: 978-09735379-3-2.**

THE BOOK OF LIGHT: THE NATURE OF GOD, THE STRUCTURE OF CONSCIOUSNESS, AND THE UNIVERSE WITHIN YOU

The Book of Light shows you the complete truth about God, the universe, and you. Within the grounded and elegant pages of this book you will find answers to top level theological/cosmological questions like "What is the nature of God and consciousness?", "What is the nature of the physical universe?", "What is our highest purpose?", "What is our essential nature?" and more. If you ever thought that spiritual enlightenment required sacrifice, strength, or years of effort, if you think that only "the special/the chosen/the few/the evolved" get to be "enlightened/saved/go to heaven," if you think ego has anything to do with enlightenment at all, think again. Remember the simple and glorious truth of your divinity. Read *The Book of Light* and find the divinity within you. **ISBN: 978-09738555-2-4.**

THE BOOK OF THE TRIUMPH OF SPIRIT: THE NEW AGE/NEW ENERGY TAROT SYSTEM

The Lightworker's Tarot system. The Book of the Triumph of Spirit is a book of Tarot. In this book, Michael Sharp recovers the western Tarot system as the quintessential tool for rapid enlightenment and empowerment. Several restrictive traditions are dropped and several cards are renamed in order to present the Tarot in pristine purity and power. As we remember our divinity, *The Fool* becomes *Joyful*. As we remember our purpose, *Judgment* gives way to *Redemption*. As *Initiation* progresses, *Death* is overcome. The book includes a complete set of the revolutionary *Halo/Sharp* Tarot deck. You may preview the full deck by visiting the Avatar website. www.avatarpublication.com. **ISBN: 978-09738555-8-6 (includes cards).**

MY MYSTICAL BIG TOE: A STRONG THEORY OF CONSCIOUSNESS AND CREATION

For too long, science and spirituality have stood at odds with each other. The two, we are told, are incompatible. Science is objective, while spirituality is subjective. Scientific truths are empirical while spiritual truths are experiential. They are two sides of a continuum with no possibility of reconciliation. But what if that is not true?

What if science and spirituality are compatible? What if they could be brought together into a logical, productive, and mutually beneficial synthesis? This is exactly what is suggested in this booklet by Dr. Sharp, who not only puts forward a workable synthesis (i.e., a "strong theory of consciousness"), but also unequivocally calls for a paradigm shift to a new, spiritually sophisticated Noetic science. The evidence against the old Newtonian, materialist paradigm is overwhelming and the shift is past due. Read *My Mystical Big Toe* and discover the bright future of science, technology, and spirituality. **ISBN: 978-1-897455-66-1.**

CHILDREN'S BOOKS BY MICHAEL SHARP

VAYDA JAYNE BEAN

Vayda Jayne Bean has some words she will share.
It's time we all learned
that monsters don't scare.
It's time we all saw
the big light that's inside.
It's time that we all threw our hearts open wide.

**Let Vayda Jayne Bean teach your Indigo or
Crystal about The Light
that's inside us all**

ISBN: 978-0-9780969-5-3
ISBN: 978-1-8974556-9-2 (eBook)
ISBN: 978-1-897455-70-8 (Dark skinned character)
ISBN: 978-1-897455-71-5 (Dark skinned eBook)

OTHER AVATAR BOOKS

THE BOOK OF SECRETS: BREAKING THE CHAINS OF YOUR FINANCIAL AND SPIRITUAL BONDAGE—ED RYCHKUN

Have you ever wondered why life is so difficult? Have you ever wondered why the treadmill never stops? Have you ever wondered why, no matter how much you work, the money always seems to flow away? Then meet Tom and Pam Doubtful, two happy light beings incarnated on earth and trapped in a matrix of commercial and spiritual illusion that has siphoned their energy, consumed their essence, and left them scrambling to break free of enthrallment. Travel with them now on their journey of freedom as they uncover the secrets of the deception. Share with them as they lift *The Veil* in order to learn who they really are. Walk with them as they break the chains of their bondage, uncover the secrets of their deception, and emerge into the bright light of the prosperity of God and Spirit that is their birthright. **ISBN: 978-0-9780969-2-2.**

THE SECRET LITTLE BOOK:
A NEW AGE PRESCRIPTION FOR A
GREAT LIFE—ED RYCHKUN

The Secret Little Book is the executive summary of ascension and everyone's ascension manual. In an informal style and easy voice, Ed Rychkun, former business executive and now ascending human, presents the essential concepts and ideas, practices and perspectives, that you will need in order that you may "catch the wave" and ascend with the planet. Keep the *Little Book* in your back pocket and take it out whenever you or someone else needs a reminder or explanation. A perfect how-to manual for vibrational ascension. **ISBN: 978-0-9780969-2-2**.

JESUS TAUGHT IT, TOO! THE EARLY
ROOTS OF THE LAW OF
ATTRACTION—PHILIP F. HARRIS

In Jesus Taught It, Too!, Philip Harris demonstrates how Christ himself taught of universal love, prosperity, and creative abundance. Using quotes taken directly from The Good Book itself, Harris clearly shows Jesus' understanding of the *Law of Attraction*. The book goes beyond current understanding of *The Law of Attraction* and emphasizes the spirituality and love behind it all. An excellent contribution to our growing collective understanding of the spiritual operation of this great universe. **ISBN 978-0-9780969-6-0.**

INDEX

Tune in.

Turn on.

Power up!